Rihanna

THE ONLY GIRL
IN THE WORLD

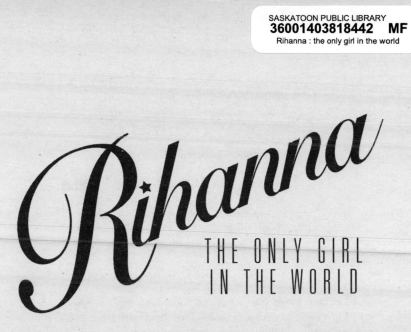

Rihanna

THE ONLY GIRL IN THE WORLD

SARAH OLIVER

JOHN BLAKE

Published by John Blake Publishing Ltd,
3 Bramber Court, 2 Bramber Road,
London W14 9PB, England

www.johnblakepublishing.co.uk

www.facebook.com/johnblakepub   facebook

twitter.com/johnblakepub   twitter

First published in paperback in 2011

ISBN: 978 1 84358 423 0

British Library Cataloguing-in-Publication Data:
A catalogue record for this book is available from the British Library.

Design by www.envydesign.co.uk

Printeed and bound by CPI Group (UK) Ltd, Croydon, CR0 4YY

1 3 5 7 9 10 8 6 4 2

Papers used by John Blake Publishing are natural, recyclable products made
from wood grown in sustainable forests. The manufacturing processes
conform to the environmental regulations of the country of origin.

Every attempt has been made to contact the relevant copyright-holders,
but some were unobtainable. We would be grateful if the
appropriate people could contact us.

Dedicated with love to
Rob, Rick, Sim and Jonny

ABOUT THE AUTHOR

Sarah Oliver is a celebrity journalist whose favourite Rihanna singles are 'Hate That I Love You', 'Take A Bow' and 'Only Girl (In the World).' You can follow Sarah on Twitter: http://Twitter.com/SarahOliverAtoZ

This book will refer to our favourite Bajan (Barbadian) singer and performer as Robyn, Rihanna and RiRi!

Other books by Sarah Oliver:

Superheroes vs Supervillains A–Z
Justin Bieber A–Z
The Wanted A–Z
One Direction A–Z
Taylor Lautner A–Z
Robert Pattinson A–Z
The Completely Unofficial *Glee* A–Z

1988: A STAR
IS BORN

Rihanna was born on 20 February 1988 at the Queen Elizabeth Hospital in Saint Michael, Barbados. Saint Michael is on the southwest part of Barbados and is one of eleven parishes. She was the first child of Monica and Ronald Fenty and was loved by her entire extended family. By then, her parents had been married for three years and they gave her the name Robyn Rihanna Fenty.

On the day she came into the world, Kylie Minogue's 'I Should Be So Lucky' was at No. 1 in the UK, and Exposé's 'Seasons Change' was No. 1 in the US.

Robyn is the female form of the name Robert and means 'bright fame'. It turned out to be an appropriate name for their beautiful baby girl. The meaning of Rihanna is 'sweet basil'. Rihanna was known as Robyn throughout her childhood, and her family and friends still call her by this name. When her singing career was about to take off, she decided to use her middle name, Rihanna. If she is out and about today and hears someone shout 'Robyn!', she might turn around to see if they are talking to her. When people shout 'Rihanna!' at her, it rarely registers; people do this all the time, and sometimes she forgets they may be talking to her, because her family, friends, crew, dancers and all those close to her call her Robyn.

When she was growing up, her mum Monica was an accountant and her father Ronald worked as a warehouse supervisor, although they both changed their jobs as she got older. They lived in a small house on Westbury New Road in Bridgetown. Bridgetown is the capital of Barbados, and Rihanna's house was only minutes away from the Kensington Oval cricket ground and the Deep Water Harbour, which is the international seaport of Barbados.

She soon became a big sister when her brother Rorrey was born, in November 1990. (If you want to, you can follow Rorrey on Twitter – just go to twitter.com/RorreyFenty.) From a young age, Rorrey and Rihanna spent a lot of time on the beaches near their home. They were just a short walk away from the idyllic Brandons beach, and Brighton, Paradise and Batts Rock beaches were also nearby. Their father taught them how to catch fish, and they had lots of cousins to play with. Rihanna told the *Sunday Herald Sun*: '[The house] where I lived in Saint Michael was literally 30 metres from the beach... it was perfect – a paradise – and we took it for granted. Basically, we woke up on a vacation every day.'

They got another brother in April 1997, when little Rajad was born. Rihanna loved mothering him, as she was nine years old when he was born, so he made the perfect doll for her to play with.

The girl who grew up in the house opposite was very close to Rihanna when they were growing up, and even now still lives in the same house with her family. Growing up, Rihanna and Shakira shared a special bond, and people could have mistaken them for sisters because of the amount of time they spent playing together. Rihanna might be a millionaire now, but Shakira is not, and today she works in a call centre. She has a little girl called Elisha and lives with her mum.

Rihanna, Rorrey and Rajad had a different ancestry to most of their friends when they were growing up, because their mother's side of the family originally came from Guyana in South America, while their father's relatives came from Barbados and Ireland. They were paler than the other kids, and Rihanna in particular was bullied by some of the children at her school: they liked to say she was white. Rihanna admitted to *Allure* magazine: 'I was a little confused as a kid, because I grew up with my mum, and my mum is black. So I was cultured in a very "black" way. But when I go to school, I'm getting called "white". They would look at me and would curse me out. I didn't understand. I just knew I saw people of all different shades and I was light. Now I'm in a much bigger world.'

Rihanna and Rorrey might have liked a lot of the same things when they were growing up, but it was Rihanna who had a passion for singing. She would lie on her bed and sing her favourite songs. Her father first caught her singing to herself when she was three years old, using her hairbrush as a microphone.

By the time she was six, Rihanna had decided that when she grew up she wanted to be a singer, and she would sing and perform whenever she could. She would perform for her cousins when they visited her, for her toys and even for the pillows on her bed. Her neighbours could hear her singing in the shower, and they gave her the nickname 'Robyn Red Breast' because she was always singing, like a bird. Her favourite songs were 'Saving All My Love For You' by Whitney Houston, and 'A Whole New World' from Disney's *Aladdin*. When she was seven, her family and neighbours realised that she had an exceptional voice talent, and her father thought that she had inherited her musical genes from his parents, who were good singers (Ronald and Monica were in no way singers themselves!).

Singing helped keep Rihanna's mind off her troubles. She might have had fun playing with Rorrey, but sometimes at night she would lie in bed and try to stop herself from drifting off to sleep: she was scared of what her father would do to her mother if she herself went to sleep.

During one violent row, Rihanna tried to stop Ronald from hurting Monica by smashing a bottle to distract him.

She hated the fact that he hurt her mother physically as well as emotionally, and she felt she couldn't tell people what was going on, even when her father broke her mum's nose. Monica didn't go to hospital and wouldn't report what was going on to the police. Rihanna just kept her feelings locked deep inside herself, and vowed never to marry someone violent. She didn't even cry, although she was hurting very badly inside.

When she turned eight, things got really bad for Rihanna, and she suffered from terrible headaches. She was taken to see the doctor, who tried to find out the cause, and for a while they thought she might have a brain tumour because she was in so much pain. It turned out that the headaches were caused by the stress Rihanna was under, because of the arguments and fights her parents were having, but of course no-one knew that at the time.

Her father was addicted to crack cocaine, and this caused many arguments and fights between her parents. He would disappear into the bathroom for ages, and little Rihanna didn't understand what was going on. When she was nine, she caught him smoking crack and told her mum. She had peered through a gap, saw him taking it and was terribly scared, because she knew he was doing something wrong. Both Rihanna and her mother cried in desperation at the situation. Today, Rihanna's dad greatly regrets what he put his family through, but at the time he would disappear for days when he was on drugs, leaving Monica to look after Rihanna and her brothers on her own. Monica kicked him out of the house a few times because of his drug-taking and the violence he inflicted on her.

Monica used to think that Ronald might end up living like a homeless man because of his drug-taking. His habit was well known and people would call him a 'parrow', which means 'freeloader' and 'junkie'. In Barbados, this is one of the worst names you can be called by people you know. The wider Bajan community had no respect for him, and just saw him as a waste of space.

In some ways Rihanna now feels sorry for her father, because he grew up knowing what it's like to be beaten by someone who is supposed to love you. When he was a young boy, his stepfather would beat him, and his mother didn't prevent it. This resulted in Ronald feeling some resentment towards Monica and women in general. In a way he punished his wife for his mother's mistakes. Rihanna knows what happened to her father as he was growing up, but she feels that doesn't excuse what he did to her mum.

When Rihanna was fourteen, her mum and dad divorced. Almost immediately, Rihanna's headaches stopped, and she could just get on with enjoying life without worrying about what was going to happen next. Monica was the best mum Rihanna could have asked for, and although she struggled to make ends meet at times, she always put Rihanna, Rorrey and Rajad first. She didn't let them know how poor they were, and would still find the money for Rihanna to have a perm every month, no matter what. Although her mum didn't realise it at the time

6

when she split up with Rihanna's father, her daughter felt a huge sense of relief.

Monica is the person that Rihanna is closest to in the whole world. She has influenced her a great deal, and Rihanna wouldn't be the woman she is today without her. When she was growing up, people would tell Rihanna that she looked like her mother, but she never believed them and would pull a face. Back then, she didn't want to look like Monica, but now she is proud to take after her, and when Rihanna sees herself on TV she can see the resemblance. She uses the same facial expressions as Monica sometimes and knows that she's just like her mum.

While Rihanna was attending Charles F. Broome Memorial School, a primary school ten minutes away from her home, she continued to dream about being a professional singer. She didn't just want to be famous in Barbados, though: she wanted to become an international superstar. She kept her dreams to herself, of course, but would pray to God that one day she would be able to tour the world. She was quite body conscious for a girl of her age and when she was eight, she decided that she didn't look right: she was eager to have curves like her mom and told Monica that she wanted 'triangular' thighs like her. Also, she adored wearing pink clothes so much that people gave her the nickname 'Pinky'.

Rihanna loved dancing as well as singing, and many people thought she would become a dancer. She was quite open about her love of dancing, whereas she kept relatively quiet about her singing at school. Every day she would go to her cousin, who was a teacher at Charles F. Broome Memorial School, and ask if she could borrow her classroom at lunchtime. Every lunchtime she would be in there, practising singing and dancing with her 'Barbie Doll Group' as they listened to the radio. Rihanna was their choreographer and they would copy her dance moves. They would all have perfume on because they liked to smell good, and wearing perfume made them feel grown-up.

Rihanna loved sport too and was in the Red House school team. Her teacher cousin, who she called 'Auntie', was in the Blue House. Rihanna would tease 'Auntie' every day, because she was convinced that her house were going to win whenever there was a sporting event. Even when they didn't, she would still say that Red House was better than Blue! Her cousin, 'Auntie', still works at the school and teaches one of the reception classes.

Rihanna and her one female cousin grew up with 15 boys in the family, so she was always a bit of a tomboy. However, she became interested in make-up and would ask her mum for advice, because Monica had changed jobs and was now a make-up advisor in a department store.

Make-up had fascinated Rihanna from an early age, but she was never allowed to wear it because she was too young. As soon as her mum left for work, though, she'd sneak a look at her make-up collection and experiment all she wanted, without getting caught. It was through watching her mum apply her make-up every day that Rihanna discovered how to do her own make-up. She says the best make-up advice she ever got from her mum was how to do her lips without showing the lip-liner. At the same time, she also learned about different perfumes and what she should do to look after her skin: she knows that getting plenty of sleep and drinking lots of water helps her skin look refreshed.

When Rihanna was four years old, she got into big trouble: she used her mum's nail varnish to give herself colourful drawn-on bracelets up her arm, and then poured what was left into her brother's toy builder's hat. She didn't realise that the nail varnish wouldn't come off for ages beca use they didn't have any remover!

When she got older, Rihanna moved to Combermere School, one of the top high schools in Barbados. In her spare time she would sell things from a stall outside a shop. She would find items that people might want – such as gorgeous scarves, stylish hats and accessories – and sell them to passers-by. At school Rihanna sold sweets to the other students and made a little money that way; she would also braid girls' hair for cash.

She wasn't interested in acting in school plays or anything like that while in high school, and instead concentrated on singing and doing well in class. Her teacher Mrs Goring told 4Music: 'She was a well-behaved student, who did her work well, never got into trouble.' She did join in, though, if the whole class was misbehaving – of course, she wasn't good 100 per cent of the time! Her teacher thought she was going to be a model, because she moved like one every time she walked down the corridor, and she was always one of the best dressed whenever there was a party.

As well as singing and dancing, whenever she had the chance Rihanna wrote poetry. She then began penning song lyrics, and was inspired by reggae artists such as Spice Cartel, Damian Marley and Sizzla, as well as the pop and R&B music of Whitney Houston, Beyoncé and Mariah Carey. For a time her mum ran a reggae club, which meant Rihanna was surrounded by music; she also loved listening to songs on the radio.

While at school, Rihanna enrolled in the Cadet Corp, a sub-military programme. The singer Shontelle was her drill sergeant back then, and Rihanna wanted to be the best cadet. She gave it everything she had, and being a tomboy certainly helped, because she didn't care how hard it got or how much Shontelle and the other drill sergeants pushed her.

Things changed when she met Melissa…

Melissa Forde moved to Rihanna's high school when she was fourteen, and the two quickly became best friends. Becoming friends with Melissa made Rihanna more interested in fashion and make-up, as Melissa was by no stretch of the imagination a tomboy. Every Friday, Rihanna, Melissa and their group of friends would have sleepovers, then head for the beach on Saturday or go shopping. In the evening they'd make their way to the club 'The Boatyard' to dance.

Her new best friend wasn't afraid to push the boundaries, and wore make-up to school, even though this wasn't allowed. Her hair was dyed blonde, which made her stand out because the other black girls in the school had dark hair. She would hang around at Rihanna's house and the two of them would look at Melissa's older sister's magazines for fashion advice. It wasn't long after she met Melissa that Rihanna decided she didn't want to be a tomboy cadet any more – she wanted to start acting like a girl.

RiRi told *Vogue*: 'When I was 14 and first started going out, I always wanted to be the opposite of everyone else. So I would go to the club in a polo T-shirt and pants and sneakers and a hat on backward, just so I would not be dressed like other girls.

'And I got desperate for things that weren't available in Barbados. I would cut things out of magazines. I was obsessed with creating a visual with clothing, and the way things are combined.'

Rihanna's first relationship with a boy was in high school. She confessed to *Rolling Stone*: 'My first kiss was in high school, and it was the worst thing ever. He pretty much dumped his entire saliva glands into my mouth. It traumatized me. I didn't kiss [again] for, like, ever.'

Melissa is still Rihanna's best friend to this day. They are so close that they have each other's birth dates as tattoos on their shoulders, and can tell each other everything. Nowadays Melissa is RiRi's official 'personal assistant' and so she travels everywhere with her, gives her fashion advice, helps Rihanna to organise her time, and is often her sounding board when she has an idea about something. When she has boyfriend issues she can count on Melissa to be there for her and help her through it. Melissa didn't have a problem about leaving her own family and friends behind in Barbados because she knows how much Rihanna relies on her. In fact, Melissa is one of only a handful of people Rihanna can trust 100 per cent.

FIRST PERFORMANCE

When she was fifteen Rihanna decided to enter a talent show at her school. She might have been singing from when she was three years old, but she had always kept it a secret from the kids at school. Her family had been encouraging her because she was really good, and so Rihanna decided to go for it. She was the youngest girl in the competition but her voice more than made up for it: the other girls might have been two years older but they weren't as talented as Rihanna. She sang 'Hero' by Mariah Carey and owned the stage. Indeed, she wasn't put off by the number of people in the auditorium and walked around with confidence. 'Hero' is a difficult song to sing, but Rihanna wanted to perform a challenging number rather than an easy one. If you haven't seen the video of her performance, you can check it out on YouTube. Back then, she never even thought about having a singing coach, but she still managed to hit the high notes.

When it was announced that Rihanna was the winner she couldn't believe it; she was overjoyed. Her family and friends were very proud of her, and the people in the auditorium felt blessed that they had seen her first big performance on a stage. Winning the competition made her even more determined to be a worldwide recording artist one day.

The following year she won the Miss Combermere Beauty Pageant, which Melissa helped organise, but singing was still her main focus. She might have had the looks to become a model, but Rihanna wanted more than that. She started making demos during the school holidays in the hope that they would lead to her securing a record deal one day. Her mum knew she was passionate about singing, but always told her that school had to come first. She made it clear that she would only let Rihanna drop out of school if she got a recording contract with a record label. Even when Evan signed her up at the age of 15, Monica still made her daughter stay on at school until the time was right: she wanted Rihanna to get her qualifications.

The main things that Monica taught Rihanna and her brothers when they were growing up were to be fearless and to take responsibility for their own actions. She might still live in Barbados, but Monica visits Rihanna in the US as often as possible. What's more, she is a great cook, and Rihanna loves it when she gets to eat one of her mum's home-cooked meals. Rihanna is also close to her cousin Noella, who visits whenever she can.

Rihanna might be a big star but her father still has to work for a living. He is no longer a warehouse supervisor, and instead sells things from the back of his car. It is thought that Rihanna hasn't helped him out financially just in case it gets him involved in drug use again. He has been 'clean' for years now, and everyone in the family wants him to stay that way.

Ronald's mum Betty is very proud of her granddaughter, as are her other grandparents. Clara Brathwaite is the name of Monica's mum, and granddaughter and grandmother are very close. When Clare was celebrating 50 years of being married to her husband Lionel in April 2009, Rihanna made sure she flew over for the family party in Barbados. She wouldn't have missed her grandparents' celebration for the world.

Rihanna is so busy that she can only visit Barbados a couple of times a year, but she flies her family out to wherever she happens to be regularly. She speaks to her mum on the phone all the time, at least once a day, and keeps in contact with her brothers too. Rorrey is now studying to be an architect, and it looks as if Rajad will be working on something to do with computers when he's older.

Over the years Rihanna's relationship with her father has been strained, but he has tried to give her advice at times. Back in 2007 he talked to her about drugs and the harm they can cause. Drugs tore their family apart, and they were a major part of his life for over twenty years before he eventually kicked the habit. He actually started taking them when he was fourteen years old and still at school, and was a user when he first met Rihanna's mum.

Of course Rihanna knew what drugs did to a person, having seen the effects of her father's addiction, but she didn't know what taking them was like firsthand. Ronald wanted to make sure it stayed that way, too – he didn't want his daughter going off the rails like some other young stars. After they talked, Rihanna reassured him she wouldn't be following in his footsteps. She is far too clever to do drugs!

Rihanna might be a big star now, but nothing has changed: she is still the girl from Barbados with a big heart. She doesn't flaunt her celebrity status and enjoys tucking into boiled eggs and the other foods she ate while growing up.

Ronald insists that he doesn't want any of Rihanna's money and he just wants to be part of her life. Sometimes he wishes he could be by her side at awards shows, but he's happy watching her on TV and seeing her whenever he can. He loves it when she rings and asks him to visit her.

At times Ronald and Rihanna have had a rocky relationship. In 2009 she fell out with him when he was visiting her in Los Angeles. He drank too much and rowed with her brother, so Rihanna simply decided that enough was enough, and had her father sent home. The two of them have mended their relationship now; they don't see each other that much, because Ronald still lives in Barbados and Rihanna doesn't have much time off from her hectic schedule, so when she does visit, she only has time to see him briefly, if at all. He has a daughter and son from another relationship, but they are shielded from the media.

After Rihanna was beaten up by her boyfriend, Chris Brown, in February 2009, her father found it hard to look at the shocking photos of her face; he couldn't even give his daughter a hug or comfort her because he was over 3,000 miles away. Ronald pitied Chris, because he had made such a huge mistake and had ruined things for himself: people would always remember and Chris would never be able to escape what he had done. Ronald knew this because of what happened in his own relationship with Monica.

ONE CHANCE
TO IMPRESS

Rihanna might have won the school talent contest as a solo artist, but she felt that she would have more chance of success if she joined forces with two friends. Girl groups were huge at the time – from Destiny's Child and TLC in the US, to the Sugababes and Girls Aloud in the UK – the music world was loving girl groups.

Rihanna and her unnamed group managed to find out through a friend that a New York music producer called Evan Rogers was holidaying in Barbados with his wife, who is Bajan. He visited family in Barbados every year, and was always on the lookout for talented singers. Rogers asked his associates on the island to tell him if they spotted any potential recording artists and one such friend suggested he allow Rihanna and her friends to audition for him.

Being informed that a music producer wanted to meet her was a massive deal for Rihanna, because she knew she would have one chance to impress him. She had to make sure the girls in her group were well rehearsed, looked good and were vocally ready. They didn't have much time to prepare: Rogers was on holiday and would soon be flying back to New York.

Evan Rogers remembers the audition as if it was yesterday. He told *Kurama* magazine: 'I thought Rihanna was a star from the moment she sang for me. She had a presence when she walked into the room. Her voice was raw but distinctive – and she wanted this career more than anything. I signed her without any hesitation. A true star is obvious to me from the moment they walk into a room. I could never have predicted how huge she would become, but I always believed she was a star from day one.'

During their audition the group sang 'Emotion' by Destiny's Child, but Evan didn't watch or listen to the other girls, just the shy girl with the beautiful voice. Rihanna might have been lacking in confidence but she impressed him very much. Rihanna was such a great singer that he chose to sign her as a solo artist, because he didn't think she needed the other girls.

When Evan's musical partner Carl Sturken heard Rihanna sing for the first time he was just as captivated, and the two producers wanted her to be the first artist on their SRP label. They asked Rihanna to come back a few days later with her mum, so they could discuss things and decide what they needed to do next.

Her two school friends didn't kick up a fuss and to this day they have remained silent, even though they could have made a lot of money by selling their stories to the press.

FACT FILE – EVAN ROGERS AND CARL STURKEN

Evan Rogers and Carl Sturken are a team of Grammy-nominated producers and songwriters who have been working in the music business for more than 20 years. They were in the same band when they were younger, and would play gigs all over the place. While they were performing in Barbados, both Rogers and Sturken fell in love with Bajan women, married them and decided to become session musicians in New York. Evan got a solo deal and started writing and producing tracks for other artists. Most of the time, Evan came up with the lyrics and Carl would pen the music.

To date they have worked on a series of albums that have sold more than 70 million copies. Over the years they have worked with Rod Stewart, Donny Osmond, Kelly Clarkson, 'N Sync, Christina Milian, Anastacia, Jessica Simpson and many more big names. In 2005 they decided to create their own record label called SRP – Syndicated Rhythm Productions – and Rihanna was the first artist they signed. They have written and produced many of Rihanna's biggest hits over the years.

Rihanna knew she would eventually have to move to the US, but she stayed in Barbados for another year. She went to school with her friends, studied and tried to act like a normal schoolgirl, but it was very hard. All she wanted to do was sing, but her mum made sure RiRi kept her feet firmly on the ground.

In the holidays she would fly out to Stamford, Connecticut, with Monica to record her demo in Evan Rogers' studio. Shortly after she turned 16 she moved out there permanently, leaving her mum and the rest of the family behind in Barbados. Evan welcomed Rihanna into his home and introduced her to his family; she lived with Evan and his wife and family while he and Carl Sturken put the finishing touches to the demo, before sending it out to labels they thought might be interested.

The first label to respond was Def Jam, who simply loved Rihanna's demo. Other labels were interested in her, but from the beginning it was clear that Def Jam were the keenest. Rihanna was only 16 but they saw that she had huge potential. They wanted to meet her and find out what she was like performing live.

Even though record labels were interested, Rihanna was still nervous – after all, she had to perform well, otherwise she could end up returning to Barbados a failure. Those classmates who had bullied her for being pale would have loved to get the opportunity to tease her about her big dreams being over.

Rihanna might have been 16 and far away from home, but there was no way she was going to mess it up. When she found out that the man she had to impress was Jay-Z she got even more nervous, because she had never met anyone that famous before. He may have liked the demo but she knew any subsequent success depended on her performance.

Rihanna revealed to *Singers' Room* magazine: 'I was in the lobby, shaking! I saw just a little bit of Jay's face down the hall and I had never met a celebrity, and to meet a celebrity who's also the president of the label, that was crazy!'

As soon as Jay-Z came to introduce himself and took her into his office, she started to relax, though. She could see that he wanted her to succeed, not fail. Rihanna chose to sing Whitney Houston's 'For the Love of You', 'Pon de Replay' and 'The Last Time' as these three songs showed off the different styles of music she could do. Jay-Z would already be very familiar with 'For the Love of You' but the other two tracks were completely new, having been written especially for Rihanna by Evan Rogers and Carl Sturken.

Jay-Z was joined by Def Jam CEO L.A. Reid; they were both overwhelmed by Rihanna's talent and wouldn't let her leave until she signed a contract. When she had finished singing, Jay-Z nodded towards her and said, 'We're interested.'

Rihanna will never forget that moment.

The pair didn't want to let her out of their sight because they knew that she had other meetings planned. In fact, they had their lawyers work on the contract while they waited, and it was finally signed around three in the morning. Rihanna was ecstatic and couldn't stop smiling as she signed her name. By the time she left it was 4.30am. It had been a long day and night, but she finally knew she was about to fulfil her dreams. She was going to be a worldwide recording artist!

Jay-Z never expected to see her sing at 4pm in the afternoon and to still be in her company in the early hours. It is very unusual to sign an artist this way, and perhaps a bit crazy too. Most people would have slept on it and met up a day or two later, but he didn't want anyone else stealing her from his label. Jay-Z knew immediately that Rihanna had the potential to be a huge star; he initially believed that 'Pon de Replay' might be too big for her, but he liked the way she performed and thought she had an amazing voice.

FACT FILE – JAY-Z AND L.A. REID

Jay-Z is a hugely successful rapper and businessman, and was president of Def Jam when Rihanna auditioned. Later, he would step down from the role to concentrate on his own label Roc-A-Fella but would continue to mentor Rihanna. Over the years he has become like a big brother to her and will always try to protect her.

Rihanna knew from the beginning that Jay-Z had her best interests at heart, and he was an expert in the music business. In fact, he has sold more than 50 million albums and has 13 Grammy Awards (five of which he had when Rihanna met him for the first time).

L.A. Reid was the CEO of Def Jam at the time of Rihanna's audition and is an award- winning record executive, producer and songwriter. During his long career he has signed many top artists including Usher, Mariah Carey, Justin Bieber, Pink, Kanye West and Avril Lavigne.

Once Jay-Z and L.A. Reid had signed Rihanna, it took three months to put together her first album before it was released. *Music of the Sun* came out on 30 August 2005 and 'Pon de Replay' was the first single. In the beginning Def Jam wanted fans to see Rihanna as 'the girl next door'.

Evan Rogers and Carl Sturken were involved in writing and producing many of the tracks chosen for the album. The band J-Status, Canadian rapper Kardinal Offishall, Jamaican singer Vybz Kartel and the musician Elephant Man all contributed as well. Because they had been working with Rihanna for over a year, they already had some of the tracks ready, so that helped to speed up the process.

The album did really well and sold 69,000 copies in the first week, which meant it reached No. 10 in the US charts – a fantastic achievement for any artist, let alone one just starting out. It has continued to sell well, and at the time of writing, more than two million copies have been sold since it was first released.

The album also performed well in the Canadian charts on its release, coming in at No. 7, and reached No. 12 in the Irish charts. It did less well in the UK, reaching No. 35.

Rihanna likened her first album to callaloo, a stew-like meal that is eaten in Barbados, announcing on its release: 'My music is mostly Caribbean beats mixed with R&B. I don't want to be pigeonholed into being just a dance artist because I can sing too. I have ballads on the album as well as upbeat tracks.'

She added: 'Music is in my DNA.'

Rihanna was the one who actually came up with the name of the album, *Music of the Sun*. She wanted the sun to be in the title because it symbolises Barbados and where she's come from, as well as herself (the track of the same name was written later on). She didn't just record songs that people had written for her; Rihanna helped write some tracks, too. She worked on the lyrics for 'Here I Go Again', 'Willing to Wait', 'Music of the Sun' and 'Now I Know'.

The tracks on the album are as follows:

1. 'Pon de Replay'
2. 'Here I Go Again' (featuring J-Status)
3. 'If It's Lovin' That You Want'
4. 'You Don't Love Me (No, No, No)' (featuring Vybz Kartel)
5. 'That La, La, La'
6. 'The Last Time'

7. 'Willing to Wait'
8. 'Music of the Sun'
9. 'Let Me'
10. 'Rush' (featuring Kardinal Offishall)
11. 'There's a Thug in My Life' (featuring J-Status)
12. 'Now I Know'

Fans loved the album but reviews from the critics were mixed. Many thought it was too similar to the music Beyoncé and Ashanti were producing. *Slant* magazine gave it two-and-a-half stars out of five and said in their review: '*Music of the Sun* gets off to an aptly breezy start with the sunshiny "Here I Go Again" and "If It's Lovin' That You Want" (co-produced by Poke & Tone), but while most of the album coasts atop its light Caribbean influence, the middle stretch of the record sinks like a Janet album. The album's final track, "Now I Know", is a too-mature, outdated, and string-laden affair for such a young, seemingly "hip" artist. Still, if inconsistency is *Music of the Sun*'s biggest flaw, Rihanna is doing quite well by today's paint-by-numbers R&B standards.'

Rolling Stone magazine gave the album the same score and commented: 'Photogenic Rihanna suggests a young Mariah Carey minus the birdcalls, and the generic vocal hiccups and frills clearly learned from American R&B often overwhelm her Caribbean charm. At 52 minutes, Rihanna's debut overstays its welcome, but the single ("Pon de Replay") justifies plenty of replays.' *Rolling Stone* went on to describe Rihanna as what 'Beyoncé might have sounded like if she had grown up in the West Indies and skipped the whole Destiny's Child thing.'

The album cover art chosen for *Music of the Sun* was typical of those released by other young artists at the time. It showed Rihanna with pink glossy lips, big gold hoop earrings and a gold sequinned jacket looking out at the camera. Only her head and shoulders were visible. She looked like the perfect all-American teen – even though she wasn't. The background was purple and pink, with her name in orange at the top above the title. It will always be a special cover to Rihanna and her family because this was her first release.

She had different cover art for the Japanese edition of the album, though. It was much simpler and Rihanna is shown standing up, leaning to the side. Her earrings don't distract your attention away from her face as they do in the original cover, and the image actually looks more like the Rihanna we now know and love.

For the cover art of 'Pon de Replay', Rihanna wears the same gold sequinned top she wore in the video, with her hair wavy, and she's smiling at someone (or something) off to her right. The background is black and there are twinkling lights up above, like stars. This time her name is at the bottom and the single's title is inside a yellow shape underneath.

For 'If It's Lovin' That You Want', Rihanna is shown in another head-and-shoulders shot. This time her body is turned away, but she has turned her face to look at the camera. She isn't smiling but she looks happy, and she's wearing another pair of large gold earrings.

The first song to be released from the album was 'Pon de Replay', and it had actually been one of four tracks on the demo that Rihanna sent out to record companies. It was released on 25 August 2005 in the UK, and a day later in the US.

Rihanna didn't like the song when she first heard it and thought it sounded a bit like a nursery rhyme. She trusted Evan Rogers and Carl Sturken, though, and the more she sang it, the more she liked it; by the time she recorded the track, she thought it was a good song.

For 'Pon de Replay' she was using the language of Barbados, where they sometimes use broken English. 'Pon' means on, 'de' means the, and 'replay' is an instruction to the DJ to put her song on repeat.

For Rihanna, filming the video was a dream come true, because this was something she had always wanted to do. It was set in a club and she had to do a lot of dancing, which she loved. The concept was that she would arrive with two friends, notice how quiet the music was and that everyone was looking bored, and ask the DJ to turn the volume up. Once the music gets louder, everyone starts dancing.

The video was directed by Little X (who now calls himself Director X), and the DJ in the video was played by DJ Cipha Sounds. Little X has directed lots of music videos, but he is best known for his work on the Sean Paul videos and R Kelly videos.

In the 'Pon de Replay' video, Rihanna wanted to show her love for her home country, and wore a ring featuring the trident head design from the Barbados national flag.

The single reached No. 2 in the US charts behind Mariah Carey's 'We Belong Together', which enjoyed 14 weeks at No. 1. At this time Mariah Carey was virtually unstoppable, so Rihanna must have felt that getting to No. 2 was like getting to No. 1; it was the highest anyone could hope to achieve because of the immense popularity of 'We Belong Together'.

Rihanna told *Glamour* magazine: 'In a matter of weeks, the first single ("Pon de Replay") went to radio. Then we shot a video, and the song just took off. I was in the Top 10 with huge artists who I looked up to. Jay-Z kept telling me, "This never happens, so don't get used to it." I saw how special that moment was.'

The single didn't just do well in the US; it also topped the music charts in New Zealand, Japan and Hungary, and landed at No. 2 in the UK and Ireland charts. For many people worldwide, it became the iconic song of summer 2005.

Because 'Pon de Replay' did so well, Rihanna was offered the opportunity to do nine shows around the US. The mini-tour was sponsored by Procter & Gamble, who wanted her to promote a new range of their deodorant brand: 'Rihanna's Secret Body Spray Tour' went to Cincinnati, Chicago, Salt Lake City, Washington D.C., Portland, Seattle, Dallas, Phoenix and Atlanta. It started on 26 October 2005 and ended on 7 December of the same year. At the beginning of each show, the audience members were given a free sample from the new range and then Rihanna would get on stage and sing six songs. Afterwards she would answer questions from the audience and sign autographs. They were nice, intimate performances, and allowed her to meet some of her fans for the first time. She hadn't been a 'celebrity' for long and so she still found it a bit strange when fans asked for her autograph and wanted to pose for photos with her.

Rihanna had worked so hard that she deserved her success, but she was so busy, she couldn't go home. She told *OK! Magazine* at the time: 'I haven't been back there [to Barbados] in so long. I live in New York now. When I do get a chance to go back to St Michael, I go to The Boatyard, which is a club. I just love it. The whole atmosphere is young and the music is really good.'

The second single to be released from Music of the Sun was 'If It's Lovin' That You Want'. Released on 28 November 2005, it failed to impress USA audiences as much as her debut single had, reaching only No. 36 in the charts. It did better in other countries, though, and got to No. 8 in Ireland, No. 9 in Australia and New Zealand, No. 11 in the UK and No. 13 in Holland.

The music video was directed by Marcus Raboy and they shot it on a beach in California. Since her first single came out, the female dancers had become friends of Rihanna's, because they had been promoting it together around the world. The men in the video were complete strangers to her, and she only met them on the day of shooting. They all got to ride jet skis and play around in the waves, just like Rihanna does with her real friends in Barbados. The trident-head symbol made a re-appearance here in three sand sculptures behind Rihanna and her dancers in the torchlit scene.

During filming, Rihanna told MTV: 'This video is about having fun, giving off the vibe of the Caribbean. We did some mermaid-looking stuff down on the sand and I'm just [performing] to the camera as if it were my boyfriend. Now we're going to do [some scenes with] the Tiki torches. It's going to be incredible!

'The song is basically telling a guy, "If it's lovin' that you want, you should make me your girl because I've got what you need."'

The third and final single from the album was called 'Let Me' and it was only released in Japan, where it charted at No. 8.

While she was promoting *Music of the Sun*, Rihanna had a cameo role in the straight-to-DVD movie, *Bring It On: All or Nothing* (2006). In addition to playing herself, she was the announcer in the scene that is the climax of the movie, where the winning cheerleading squad is revealed. Rihanna was acting in front of hundreds of people, but she didn't let it bother her. What is more, she hadn't had any time to rehearse, because she had only one day on set.

In the movie, one of the cheerleaders from the smart school complains that the other squad has won, and what she says to Rihanna is 'borderline racist' according to director Steve Rash, who talked to 4Music about it. He said he hadn't given Rihanna a line to respond with, and so she just let her body language do the talking. That impressed the director, because it takes a real actor to be able to convey a response using only their movements rather than words.

The movie starred *Heroes* actress Hayden Panettiere and Beyoncé's sister Solange Knowles, and was the second follow-up to the 2000 movie *Bring It On* starring Kirsten Dunst. Rihanna didn't see the movie as being her first big acting job because she was playing herself, but her fans loved it.

She later admitted during interviews that she was looking forward to acting in a drama, horror or action movie in the future.

Her family and friends in Barbados were very happy that Rihanna was living her dreams, but that didn't stop some people from making up lies about her. Rihanna explained to journalist Margeaux Watson from EW.com: 'When I first got signed and went back to Barbados, people started talking about it. They said, "Oh, she must've slept with Jay-Z to get her deal." That's where I first heard it. They talk s★★★ about me all the time.' It was as though they were jealous of her success and wanted to pull her down to their level.

People in the US started saying that Rihanna and Jay-Z were having a relationship, even though he was dating Beyoncé at the time. This was particularly hard for Rihanna to take, as she was only just starting out and Jay-Z was her mentor, nothing more. They had been out to dinner together, but that was work-related, and he was always at the end of the phone if she had any difficulties. Both denied being in a relationship to the press, but some people refused to let the story die and continued to make comments on internet forums.

The media seemed to suggest that Rihanna was trying to steal Jay-Z from Beyoncé, and that Beyoncé in turn was furious with Rihanna. In fact, this couldn't have been further from the truth. When Rihanna was interviewed by talk-show host Tyra Banks, she had a broken toe, so her foot was strapped up and she had to walk with a cane for support; Tyra joked that really Beyoncé had pushed her down some stairs, which made Rihanna laugh.

She had actually been on holiday, and on the first night she wanted to go to the pool – even though it was 4.30am. While rushing back to her friend's room, she managed to walk into a heavy mahogany chair and knocked her toe the wrong way.

Rihanna and Jay-Z talked about the rumours from the beginning, and he told her to try and ignore what people were saying. The more people talked about her supposed rivalry with Beyoncé, the more annoying it became. In fact the two singers get on really well, and Rihanna thinks Beyoncé is one of the sweetest people you could meet.

Even though Rihanna was busy, she still had the occasional holiday, and returned to Barbados for Christmas 2005. She enjoyed catching up with her friends and family, eating her mum's food and visiting all the places she loved to go before she was famous. She missed her music, though, and was eager to get back to recording.

2006: A GIRL LIKE ME

Just eight months after *Music of the Sun* came out, Rihanna released her second album, *A Girl Like Me*, in April 2006. Most artists wouldn't have been able to keep up with the speed at which she was working: she was writing, recording and promoting non-stop. She herself didn't mind, though, because she finally had the chance to do what she had always dreamed of doing, and for this she would work from 6am to 6pm every day.

A Girl Like Me was released first in Japan, on 19 April 2006. Five days later, it came out in the UK, and was then released in the US on 25 April. Evan Rogers and Carl Sturken wrote many of the tracks, alongside Ne-Yo, Sean Paul, producer J.R. Rotem and Stargate's production team (Tor Erik Hermansen and Mikkel Storleer Eriksen). It had a similar feel to *Music Of The Sun*, although there was a rock-influenced side to some of the tracks. Rihanna toured with Gwen Stefani in Japan to promote *Music of the Sun,* and Stefani's style of music had influenced her own work.

The album sold well worldwide, as Rihanna's fans all rushed out to buy a copy. It topped the charts in Canada and reached No. 5 in the US and UK. In its first week in the US alone, it sold 115,000 copies – almost double the sales of *Music of the Sun* in the same period, which shows just how popular Rihanna had become. It was also in the Top 10 in Australia, Belgium, Czech Republic, Hungary, Ireland, Japan, Mexico, New Zealand and Switzerland!

In order to get her second album out so quickly after *Music of the Sun*, Rihanna had to write and record tracks at the same time as promoting her first album. This was a big challenge as she was travelling all over the place. She had to spend many long nights recording, then get up early and hit the road. To succeed in this, she needed all her inner strength, and she did well not to burn herself out. Her song, 'Kisses Don't Lie', was created in Barbados, because this is where the two men who discovered her wrote it (with her help), and where she recorded the track. All in all, it took Rihanna and her team five months in total to finish the album.

Rihanna decided to give her second album the title *A Girl Like Me* because it was filled with tracks exploring her own life experiences, things that other girls of her age go through all the time. As she explained to MTV: 'Vocally I've matured so much, and lyrically I'm speaking about stuff I would never sing about [before this]. Now I'm singing about experiences that I've gone through and stuff that other 18-year-old girls go through, so it's all about progression.'

In the album Rihanna sings about the complexity of love, of secrets, the pitfalls of relationships, of being a cheat and about people trying to pull you down.

Once the album was completed, she promoted it in various different ways. She did her own tour, took part in the Australian 'Rock Tha Block Tour' alongside Jay-Z and Ne-Yo, and also became the opening act for the Pussycat Dolls' 'PCD World Tour' in their November UK concerts. On the Pussycat Dolls' tour, she would sing eleven songs at every performance before the girls took to the stage. This must have been extremely tiring, but Rihanna gave it her all. Naturally she was keen for the audience members to go home eager to buy her album *A Girl like Me*.

The tracks on the album are as follows:

1. 'S.O.S.'
2. 'Kisses Don't Lie'
3. 'Unfaithful'
4. 'We Ride'
5. 'Dem Haters' (featuring Dwane Husbands)
6. 'Final Goodbye'
7. 'Break It Off' (featuring Sean Paul)
8. 'Crazy Little Thing Called Love' (featuring J-Status)
9. 'Selfish Girl'
10. 'P.S. (I'm Still Not Over You)'
11. 'A Girl like Me'
12. 'A Million Miles Away'

13. 'If It's Lovin' That You Want (Part 2)' (featuring Cory Gunz)

For the album cover, Rihanna and her record company chose a close-up image that was very simple and showed off her natural beauty. Her hair hangs loose and free, covering part of her face, she's wearing hardly any make-up and her left hand is just about to pull her shoulder strap up. Her face is the main focus of the picture and she's standing outside, bathed in natural light. At the top of the cover are her name and the album's title.

For the limited–edition deluxe version of the album, a second cover art was released. In this image, Rihanna is standing sideways but her right hand touches the wall behind her, and she has turned her head to look at the camera. Her hair is loose again, and she is wearing some of her trademark dangly earrings and a purple, backless dress.

For the 'S.O.S.' cover, Rihanna looked sultry; she is captured sitting on the floor with her back leaning against a stone wall, and one hand fiddles with the necklace she wears. One of her fingers is underneath her white blouse and she gazes provocatively at the camera. Her hair is wavy and natural, with her right eye covered by a fringe.

Rihanna's cover art for 'Unfaithful' was taken at the same time and place as the 'S.O.S.' cover, and she wears the same white blouse, necklace and jeans. This time her arms are by her side and she gazes to the left. Her name and the single's title are much larger, though, and cover the bottom half of the image.

For the 'We Ride' cover art, Rihanna wears the same purple dress she wore for the limited- edition deluxe album cover. She is smiling and we get a sense of movement; a piece of fabric hangs behind her as if she's been dancing or running. The background is a wooden wall and this time, her name and the album's title run together across the middle of the image.

For 'Break It Off' the cover art was more important than for the other singles, because no video was released. From the cover-art image, fans would use their imagination to come up with what the video might have looked like, had it been made. The image Rihanna chose was of her wearing a long white dress (which the fans suspected might be a wedding dress), running away, with her hands hitching up the skirt of the dress to make this easier and to give the impression that she's about to do a twirl. She looks as if she is holidaying in a foreign country, with the trees and bushes in the background making it seem almost tropical.

'S.O.S.' was the first of Rihanna's singles from the second album to be released, and it reached the No. 1 spot in the US on May 13. Now she had achieved what she had always wanted: a No. 1 single!

Rihanna was surprised when she found out that she had topped the charts, because one minute the song was in the thirties and the next it was No. 1. It stayed at No. 1 for three weeks in the US but fared even better in Australia, where it was No. 1 for eight weeks. It was also No. 1 in Canada and No. 2 in the UK, Belgium, Germany and Hungary.

Both critics and fans loved the song because it sounded

more like 'Pon de Replay' and sampled the Soft Cell track, 'Tainted Love'. The writers had also cleverly added lyrics from several popular 80s songs, from Michael Jackson's 'The Way You Make Me Feel' to Kim Wilde's 'You Keep Me Hangin' On'.

Before she recorded the song, Rihanna hadn't been at all familiar with 'Tainted Love' – after all, she wasn't exposed to much 80s' music growing up in Barbados – but she had heard it a couple of times while living in the US. She was actually the second artist considered to release the track; the song had originally been given to Christina Milian, but she had decided not to record it for her third album. Rihanna may not have been the first choice to sing it, but once she sang the song she made it her own, and after three days in the studio the finished recording was ready for the album.

For this song, Rihanna filmed one main video and two additional promotional videos, one for Agent Provocateur and another for Nike. For the main video she is seen using a Nokia mobile phone and the camera zooms in on it, clearly pushing Nokia phones. For a time this resulted in MTV banning the video. Rihanna was so popular with young people that companies would pay good money for her to promote their brands in her videos. 'S.O.S.' was the first video that Rihanna did with this kind of product placement, and the money these companies gave for the privilege no doubt paid for some of the production costs.

In 2010 Rihanna spoke to *NME* about the subject of product placement: 'I don't like things to be so commercial.

I hate product placement in my videos. Videos should just tell the story of the song.

'With product placement, it becomes this big ad campaign. I just don't like that. Sometimes we have to [use products in music videos], for whatever political reason, but it's never my first choice.'

As well as being Rihanna's biggest song to date, 'S.O.S.' won her a Billboard Music Award for 'Hot Dance Airplay Song of the Year' and a MuchMusic Video Award for 'Best International Artist Video'. All those people who had claimed she was a one-hit wonder after 'Pon de Replay' was released turned out to be wrong. Rihanna was here to stay!

The ballad 'Unfaithful' was next to be released, and this track was written by Ne-Yo, Tor Erik Hermansen and Mikkel Storleer Eriksen. Rihanna had wanted to work with Ne-Yo for a while because she had been amazed by the track he wrote for Mario. She thought 'Let Me Love You' was awesome, and when he visited her in the studio for the first time, they chatted about doing something together. She already had her tracks for the first album but once that was out of the way, they started thinking about a song for *A Girl Like Me*. That song was 'Unfaithful', a different style of song to anything Rihanna had done before. A beautiful ballad rather than an up-tempo number, the song became one of her favourites.

'Unfaithful' is about a woman who is cheating on her boyfriend. Rihanna admitted that she drew on a personal experience that she had when she was fourteen, but explained that in her case the relationship wasn't physical. In an interview with MTV, she confessed: 'I'm referred to as a murderer in that song, meaning, I'm taking this guy's life by hurting him, cheating on him. He knows, and it makes him feel so bad. It's killing him to know that another guy is making me happy. I love that song because we always put it out there that guys cheat and finally someone put it in perspective: Girls cheat too.'

'Unfaithful' reached No. 6 in the US on July 22 and got to No. 2 in the UK, Ireland, Australia, Austria, Germany and Norway.

The video for 'Unfaithful' was directed by Anthony Mandler and was set in a restaurant and on a stage. A movie of the same name featuring Richard Gere and Diane Lane is said to have been a source of inspiration for the video concept.

In the video Rihanna is sitting in a restaurant when she is passed a note, written by her lover, while her boyfriend is away from the table. Later, she texts her lover and goes out to meet him while her boyfriend sleeps. There are scenes of Rihanna singing next to a pianist on a stage and he is revealed to be her lover. After finishing their 'performance', Rihanna leaves and her boyfriend meets her. She can't help but cry as she hugs him.

The same month that 'Unfaithful' was released, Rihanna hit the road and performed her first proper concert tour. It was called the 'Rihanna: Live in Concert Tour' and altogether she played over 30 dates in the US and Canada, with one very special concert in Jamaica as part of the Red Stripe Reggae Sumfest. On selected dates she was joined by Sean Paul, Ciara, J-Status, Trey Songz, Yung Joc, Field Mob and Jeannie Ortega; they either performed beforehand as her supporting act or joined her onstage for her collaboration tracks.

Performing on stage every night gave Rihanna such a buzz that she couldn't wait to do another tour!

'We Ride' was the third single to be released from the album, but it failed to make the Top 100 in the US charts when released in August 2006. It charted at No. 4 in Finland, No. 7 in Germany, No. 17 in the UK and Ireland, and No. 24 in Australia.

Rihanna had been optimistic and thought it would do well, because fans had seemed to love the song; before its release it had been her third most downloaded track on iTunes. She told MTV: '"We Ride" is about this guy saying over and over again, "When we ride, we ride, we're gonna be together until the day that we die" – promising all these things and then it turns out he broke all of his promises, which is sad – but it's summer and I don't care if you wanna do that and be ugly and unfaithful, then I can just do my thing, chill with my girls and have fun.

'That's what summers are all about. And every summer you remember a certain relationship and there's always a song to connect to that. So "We Ride" is just one of those songs.'

'Break It Off' was released in December 2006 but it didn't have a video. It was the final release from the album, *A Girl Like Me*. The song was written by Sean Paul, Rihanna, Donovan Bennett and Kirk Ford. Sean Paul sang the majority of the single with Rihanna singing other parts of the track.

When Rihanna performed the song live she generally did so as part of a medley, because her bit of the track lasts less than two minutes.

'Break It Off' reached No. 9 in the US charts and No. 19 in the Canada charts – a fantastic achievement, considering there was no accompanying video. Fans were disappointed by Def Jam and Atlantic Records' decision not to film one, but Rihanna was too busy planning her next album.

GOOD GIRL
GONE BAD

Rihanna began 2007 by collaborating with the Jamaican band J-Status on their track, 'Roll It'. This was an updated version of 'Roll It Gal', which was written by Shontelle Layne and Sheldon Benjamin for the singer Alison Hinds. Layne and Benjamin changed the lyrics especially for J-Status and Rihanna (Shontelle helped with the vocals, too).

J-Status and Shontelle were acts signed to SRP, Evan Rogers and Carl Sturken's label. J-Status stands for 'people of Jamaican Status'. The band first worked with Rihanna on her *Music of the Sun* album, providing the male vocals for 'Here I Go Again'. 'Roll It' was the first single from their debut album, *The Beginning*.

It was released in Germany, Finland, Switzerland and Portugal, but only made the Top 10 in Finland, where it got to No. 8.

Around this time, Rihanna was still a single lady and went on a date with *Transformers*' actor Shia LaBeouf, but they didn't connect in the right way. Shia explained to *Playboy* magazine: 'It never got beyond one date. The spark wasn't there. We weren't passionate about each other in that way, so we remain friends.'

For her third album Rihanna wanted to show the world what the *real* Rihanna was like. She didn't want people to tell her how she should look, what she should sing or the kind of person she should be: she wasn't a 16-year-old girl anymore; she was a women and ready to show off her rebellious side. She didn't want to be the same-old girl next door.

When fans bought their own copies of *Good Girl Gone Bad*, they saw a new side to Rihanna, and she was glad of it. She told Bang Showbiz: '[Before *Good Girl Gone Bad* was released] I had a ridiculous schedule. It was kind of unfair. But I kept going. I was focusing on getting people to respect me as an artist, making my stamp in the industry.

'I wasn't 100% or even 75% in control of my image or my sound. I said, "If you guys keep this perfect image of me, people will never notice me." I kind of blended in. It was safe, the blonde, curly hair. It was a formula. I didn't want to be like all the other artists. I wanted to stand out. And the only way I could do that was by taking charge of my image and sound. And it worked. *Good Girl Gone Bad* was a big turning point for me.'

People think that being a world-famous singer must be the best job in the world, but it does have its downsides.

Rihanna has had to work very hard, and while growing up, she has missed out on many things that normal teenagers get to do. However, she knew she had to make sacrifices so her dreams could come true, and revealed to *GQ* magazine: 'Nothing in life comes easy. Everything comes with a sacrifice. If this is what I love to do most then I have to put up with the s★★t, that I don't love, that comes with it.'

Ne-Yo contributed to *Good Girl Gone Bad*, along with Justin Timberlake, Timbaland and Tricky Stewart, as well as Evan Rogers and Carl Sturken. Justin Timberlake wrote 'Rehab', and he told *Entertainment Weekly*: 'She's a young artist stepping into the adult world. To me, that song ("Rehab") is the bridge for her to be accepted as an adult in the music industry.'

Jay-Z, too, could see that Rihanna had changed, commenting: 'She's found her voice. That's the best thing for any label, to have an artist step in and take control of their own career – she's left the nest.' He drew comparisons with Janet Jackson's *Control*, which was the star's breakthrough album, back in 1986.

Jay-Z is Rihanna's friend as well as her mentor, and because he is famous too, he can offer her good advice about handling fame. He told journalist Margeaux Watson: 'The biggest advice I can give her is to keep her circle tight, because she can't control anything else outside of that. She can't control people's opinion of her records or what's being said on the blogs, but if she has the proper friends, she won't get caught up in the wild-child lifestyle.

47

They will bring her back [down to earth] and be like, "You might wanna pull your skirt down."'

As well as changing the type of music she wanted to make, Rihanna also altered the way she looked, and ditched the girly Caribbean style she used to have, instead picking clothes that showed off her womanly figure. She also rebelled by cutting her hair, something she had wanted to do for ages but had never been able to because the people around her liked her to have long hair. Rihanna wanted to express herself with her hair, rather than having the same style as Beyoncé and many of the other female artists who all wore their hair long and straight.

She worked with Ne-Yo again and together they wrote 'Hate That I Love You'. He also penned 'Good Girl Gone Bad', 'Question Existing' and 'Take A Bow' (for *Good Girl Gone Bad: Reloaded*). Ne-Yo gave her some singing lessons, too. She wanted to make sure that her vocals were as good as they could be, and Ne-Yo was certainly up to the challenge of teaching Rihanna. She had a raw ability but didn't understand some of the things he asked her to do, as she confessed to MTV: 'He is such a genius. I've never had vocal training so when I'm in the studio, he'll tell me how to breathe and stuff. And I'm like, "What?" Like, he'll call out these big fancy words: "OK, I want you to do staccato." And I'm like, "OK, I don't know what that is."'

Good Girl Gone Bad was released in May 2007, while *Good Girl Gone Bad: Reloaded* was released the following June. The original album was a big success for Rihanna as it sold 162,000 copies in the first week alone, and entered the US music charts at No. 2. It also topped the music charts in Europe, UK, Ireland, Canada, Hungary and Poland, and reached No. 2 in Australia and Denmark.

While writing and recording tracks for the album, Rihanna was constantly listening to *Afrodisiac* by Brandy. She loved every track on that album – there wasn't a single one that she didn't want to listen to over and over again. This made her eager to produce an album that her fans would be able to say exactly the same thing about: she wanted every track to be just as strong as the others.

Good Girl Gone Bad has a more up-tempo vibe than *A Girl Like Me* and has more pop tracks on it, without neglecting the R&B and dance elements. Before it came out, Rihanna told MTV: 'You feel different every album and [at] this stage I feel like I want to do a lot of uptempo [songs]. I want to keep people dancing but still be soulful at the same time.'

She revealed the new Rihanna to the Star Phoenix: 'I basically took the attitude of the bad girl and I really got rebellious and just did everything the way I wanted to do it – I didn't want to listen to anybody, I didn't consult with anybody. I just want to have a little more fun with my music and be a little more experimental in terms of my image and my sound. I just reinvented myself. It's all about the attitude that you take toward things. I'm not being careful, I'm just having fun – I'm taking risks because bad girls take risks.'

The tracks on *Good Girl Gone Bad* are as follows:

1. 'Umbrella' (featuring Jay-Z)
2. 'Push Up On Me'
3. 'Don't Stop the Music'
4. 'Breakin' Dishes'
5. 'Shut Up and Drive'
6. 'Hate That I Love You' (featuring Ne-Yo)
7. 'Say It'
8. 'Sell Me Candy'
9. 'Lemme Get That'
10. 'Rehab'
11. 'Question Existing'
12. 'Good Girl Gone Bad'

On the UK version, 'Cry' was added as a bonus track, and for the Japanese version, 'Haunted' was added.

The extra tracks on *Good Girl Gone Bad: Reloaded* are:

1. 'Take A Bow'
2. 'If I Never See Your Face' (with Maroon 5)
3. 'Disturbia'

The *Good Girl Gone Bad: Reloaded* album was accompanied by a DVD documentary of Rihanna performing in Manchester. It was a huge hit with fans and many outlets sold out.

For the *Good Girl Gone Bad* album cover art, Rihanna wears a white dress and leans back into the shadows, which gives the impression that she is both good (white dress) and bad (shadows). The image is taken from the side and she looks slightly downwards at the camera; her arms cross her body, with her hands placed on top of each other. Her name is written in a large green type that runs across the middle of the image, with the title in lower case white text below. The R*eloaded* version of the album uses the same image but with a green background and her name in red.

The cover for 'Umbrella' has become one of Rihanna's most iconic covers. It shows her wearing Wellington boots and holding onto her umbrella, which is the wrong way up on the floor. She's got her head back and her right hand is running through her hair. She is standing next to a pool, with a huge water swirl behind her. Her name and the title are in the top left-hand corner.

For the 'Shut Up and Drive' cover, Rihanna chose a more intimate photo of her on a purple couch, with her sweater pulled down to reveal a black bra. She's got her back to the camera, but looks back over her shoulder, and her expression is seductive. Her name is written in green, as on the album cover, and the song title is once again in lower case.

On the 'Hate That I Love You' cover, Rihanna is shown kneeling in a bedroom, looking straight at the camera. Her hair is covering her left eye and she wears a black dress that shows off her curves. Her left hand touches her right shoulder, and she's wearing black gloves. This image shows her sexy but vulnerable side. The bedcovers are yellow and the walls of the room are purple: the contrast with Rihanna's black dress makes her stand out more. Her name runs across the bottom half of the image and is in purple this time. The song title is still white, though it is now in capitals.

The cover art for 'Don't Stop the Music' was very similar to the album cover. Rihanna wears a white dress, and the background is black with a white spotlight on the singer, who is facing the camera and looking straight ahead. Her left eye is covered by her hair and she is leaning slightly on her left leg (which accentuates her curves), with her right forearm just touching her hip. Rihanna's name is in green in the top left-hand corner, with the single name in white text underneath.

For 'Take A Bow', Rihanna chose a simple image of herself with her head bowed. She isn't wearing a lot of make-up and the only jewellery she wears is a simple gold necklace and studs in her left ear (the star tattoo in her ear is also visible). Below her face is her name written in black and the song title in pink.

The 'Disturbia' cover art was also subtle, as it was just a head-on close-up of Rihanna's face. Her make-up is minimal, with nude coloured lips, and the only background that is visible is black. This is one of the least memorable of Rihanna's covers.

For 'Rehab', a more colourful cover art was chosen to reflect the desert setting of the video. Rihanna's head and shoulders are shown at an angle, with the singer looking to the right of the image. Had it been shot in black and white the image might have appeared harsh, but the colourful green shoulder straps, her sparkling, dangly earring and the green tinge as the light hits her forehead make the image feel warm and inviting. The sun is shining and the blurred backdrop adds even more colour to the image. Her name and the song's title are written in white in the bottom right-hand side of the cover.

When 'Umbrella' was released on 29 March 2007, people went crazy for the song and it soon topped the US Billboard Hot 100 charts. Altogether, it stayed at the top for seven weeks and even caused iTunes to crash at one point because so many people wanted to download it. The track was No. 1 in the UK, Ireland, Canada, Australia, Germany, France, Sweden and Switzerland. It actually stayed at the top of the UK charts for 10 consecutive weeks.

'Umbrella' might be seen as Rihanna's signature track, but it wasn't originally meant to be sung by her. The song was written and composed by producer Christopher 'Tricky' Stewart and songwriter The-Dream, who originally wanted Britney Spears to record it. When Britney's people declined on her behalf because they already had tracks for her album, they decided they wanted Mary J. Blige to record the song instead. They sent her people a copy and at the same time sent L.A. Reid a copy, then quickly found themselves part of a bidding war, because both sides wanted it. Luckily for Rihanna, Mary was too busy with her Grammy commitments to listen to the track, as she had been nominated for eight awards. Her people couldn't say they definitely wanted it until she herself had approved it, and so they had to wait for her approval.

Tricky explained what it was like to MTV: 'In a two-day period, we were in the bidding war of our lives between

Mary J. Blige's camp and Karen Kwak (Island Def Jam's executive vice president of A&R), and L.A. Reid's camp.

'At the time, if you heard Mary's name and you heard Rihanna's name, you'd want to hold out,' Stewart continued. 'Mary's coming off "Be Without You", she's nominated for all these Grammys, the whole thing. So the plan with us, really, was to hold the record to get a response from Mary. By the time L.A. Reid and his team got done beating us up, we just couldn't say no. They're calling every 20 minutes for the entire Grammy weekend. Every time we see him, everywhere we see him, they were just applying all kinds of pressure.'

Once Rihanna heard the track and was allowed into the studio to record her interpretation, she made the song completely her own with her 'ellas'. Having Jay-Z collaborating on the song moved things up another notch, and he re-wrote his rap from the original rap penned by Tricky and The-Dream. In addition to writing 'Umbrella', The-Dream was one of the writers of 'Sell Me Candy', 'Lemme Get That' and 'Breakin' Dishes' on the album.

As well as Rihanna becoming a bigger star as a result of 'Umbrella', The-Dream became much higher-profile, and he has released several albums since then, including 'The Love IV' in 2011. He has continued to write and produce great tracks with Tricky, and together they wrote the Beyoncé track 'Single Ladies', Mariah Carey's 'Touch My Body' and many more great songs.

Rihanna admits that she is grateful to have had the opportunity to record 'Umbrella' because of the boost it gave her both musically and commercially; the track also allowed her to secure a particularly lucrative endorsement deal. She told Q *Magazine*: 'I did have a deal with an umbrella company and they had a range of very good umbrellas. This is kind of weird because I grew up in Barbados and there's not a great culture of umbrellas, like there is in the UK and Europe. I guess we have the occasional storm or maybe the Caribbean is more known for its hurricanes, and an umbrella isn't going to get you very far in a situation like that. But yes, I have a few umbrellas. Maybe ten? I dunno, but I am very grateful to the umbrella for what it has done for my career.'

The video for 'Umbrella' was directed by Chris Applebaum, who had previously directed Rihanna in one of the 'S.O.S.' videos. He came up with the idea of having the singer completely covered in silver body paint after she asked him to dream up a treatment that took risks. She wanted to do something different in the 'Umbrella' video and loved the idea. A make-up artist called Pamela Neal was given the job of mixing the paint, and during the shoot it had to be be reapplied every minute. Only Rihanna, Chris and his assistant were on set during those scenes to allow her some privacy – after all, it took a lot of guts to strip naked for the cameras. After they had finished shooting it, the assistant started to cry. Chris told MTV what she said when he asked her if she was okay: 'She looked at me and said, "Chris, this is just so beautiful! I just can't believe I'm actually watching this. This is the most incredible thing

I've ever seen." And it really felt to me like we were shooting something unique at that moment.'

In the video Rihanna stands 'en pointe', which is a classical ballet technique that involves moving on the tips of the toes. This was her idea and she trained really hard so that she'd be able to do it. It's a very uncomfortable technique but Rihanna hid her pain, so you won't be able to spot it in the video.

Rihanna might have taken a risk with the 'Umbrella' video but it certainly paid off. She won Video of the Year and Monster Single of the Year at the MTV Video Music Awards in September 2007, which was a great feeling, although she did miss out on the other two awards for which she had been nominated: she was beaten by Fergie in the Female Artist of the Year category, while Justin Timberlake won the Best Direction category.

She also won the Hot Dance Airplay: Song of the Year and European Hot 100: Song of the Year awards at the Billboard Music Awards, and Most Watched Video on MuchMusic.com at the MuchMusic Video Awards in June 2008.

At the Grammy Awards in February 2008, Rihanna got the opportunity to perform 'Umbrella' and 'Don't Stop the Music' in front of some of the best performers in the world. She was thrilled to win her first Grammy for 'Umbrella' as it was named Best Rap/Sung Collaboration – she was very grateful that Jay-Z decided to collaborate with her, because otherwise she wouldn't have even been nominated. They had been up against Akon and Snoop

Dogg for 'I Wanna Love You'; Chris Brown and T-Pain for 'Kiss, Kiss'; Keyshia Cole, Missy Elliott and Lil' Kim for 'Let It Go'; and Kanye West and T-Pain for 'Good Life'. Rihanna dragged Jay-Z onstage and gave him a big hug. In her speech she said: 'Dad, I know I promised you I'd give you my first Grammy, but we're going to have to fight for this one!'

Shortly after her success with 'Umbrella', Gillette Venus Breeze named Rihanna 'Celebrity Legs of a Goddess' and they insured her legs for $1 million. She became one of their judges for a competition in the US, and she said at the time: 'I'm thrilled that Venus Breeze thinks my legs are award-worthy and I'm excited to kick off the search for the woman with the best legs in America. This contest is a fun way for women to showcase confidence, charisma and gorgeous legs on the runway.'

Nowadays she shrugs off the award Gillette gave her, because she had a deal with them and admits that they didn't pick her randomly; she was being paid to promote their brand of razor and the award ceremony was just a PR stunt. Rihanna went on to secure more endorsement deals after 'Umbrella' proved to be such a smash hit around the world.

She became the face of CoverGirl cosmetics too, and appeared in their TV advertisements. In her first one she appeared with an umbrella, asking the viewers at home, 'Wanna know what I've got on under my umbrella? It's new CoverGirl Wetslicks Fruit Spritzers with twelve delicious flavours – you get a refreshing burst of shine without all that sticky feeling. Even if it's raining, your lips will have lasting fruity shine!' At the end of the ad, she would encourage viewers to buy her album.

Over 30 top singers and bands have covered 'Umbrella' since it first came out, which is a huge compliment to Rihanna and the writing team behind the track. Chris Brown was the artist chosen to do the official remix: he altered the chorus and added some new verses. His version was called 'Cinderella Under The Umbrella'. Back then, he was attracted to Rihanna and did flirt, although things didn't go further at the time.

The media tried to suggest they were dating, and fans of both singers wanted them to hook up, but in the beginning they were just friends. Their friendship eventually developed into a romance, but first, Chris became Rihanna's best friend. She found being around him helped her forget about all her stresses and worries. He knew what it was like to be famous, and how it felt to be constantly on the move recording and promoting singles and albums. Since the time she signed her first record deal she had had to behave as an adult, looking after herself. Joking around with Chris made her remember what it was like to be a teenager, without a care in the world.

After she won her Grammy, she took Chris with her when she went back to Barbados to catch up with friends and family. At her 20th birthday party, he sang 'Happy Birthday' a capella and helped her cut the cake. They then headed to Jamaica for a well-deserved break. Rihanna was to perform at the 'Smile Jamaica Africa Unite' concert on the Saturday, but they still had loads of fun hanging out in the swimming pool of the luxurious Hilton Kingston hotel.

Being with Chris, and having the ability to express herself in her music, transformed Rihanna from the shy girl she used to be. When she first started being interviewed by journalists, she was very nervous and wouldn't know what to say. She was a shadow of herself, but as she did more and more interviews she learned how to relax and enjoy herself. Soon she didn't mind being silly and messing around – and started having a lot more fun.

The two kept on insisting in interviews that they were just the best of friends, but when Jordin Sparks gave an interview to *Young Voices* in April 2008, she revealed they were dating. She had collaborated with Chris on her track 'No Air' and Rihanna came along while they were filming the video. When Jordin was asked, 'Are Chris Brown and Rihanna dating?', she replied: 'Yeah, they are. It was really cool because I walked on the set and she was sitting there with Chris Brown and I was like, I can't believe she's here. She came and she told me that she loved "No Air" and that it was one of her favourite songs. It was really cool hearing that from one of my peers. She just wanted to support him.'

Jordin was also asked: 'Did it feel weird doing intimate scenes with Chris Brown, with his girlfriend watching you?' She laughed and admitted: 'It was hard at first, but then I said, "You know what? I have to work!" It had to look like I was in love with him, so I had to do it. Hopefully she won't kill me!'

'Shut Up and Drive' was the second single to be released

from the *Good Girl Gone Bad* album and it came out in June 2007 in the US, although European Rihanna fans had to wait until August 2007. But it wasn't as well received as 'Umbrella' had been, and only reached No. 15 in the US charts. Elsewhere it did better – it made it to No. 4 in Australia and Hungary, No. 5 in the UK and Ireland, and No. 6 in Canada, Germany and Finland.

The video was directed by Anthony Mandler (who also directed 'Unfaithful' and 'We Ride'), but this time filming took place in a junkyard in Prague in the Czech Republic. In the video, Rihanna is shown in the driving seat of a Ferrari F430, although she doesn't actually have a driving licence. The concept was that she and her friends are car mechanics and they watch two men race before Rihanna performs with her rock band.

'Shut Up and Drive' was used in the TV ad for the ninth series of *America's Next Top Model*.

When it was first released on July 4 2007, some bloggers tried to suggest that Rihanna had stolen the 'beat' of the New Order track 'Blue Monday' for 'Shut Up and Ride' without acknowledging it – in fact, the track had been lawfully sampled and credited.

The third track that Rihanna released from the album was 'Hate That I Love You' featuring Ne-Yo. It came out on 21 August 2007 and reached No. 7 in the US charts. In the UK, it only made it to No. 15, but it did better in New Zealand, where it charted at No. 6, and Sweden, where it reached No. 10; it also made No. 11 in Germany.

In Spain, Rihanna released a special version with David

Bisbal singing in Spanish; David is a Spanish pop singer. Rihanna still sings in English but her Spanish fans loved it. For three weeks, it was No. 3 in the Spanish charts. 'Odio Que Te Amo' was released in April 2008. To date, almost four million copies of this version alone have sold worldwide.

Rihanna appreciates how deep the lyrics are, and when reading them for the first time, she kept asking Ne-Yo what he was thinking while writing the song. She believes he's a very talented songwriter, and is always surprised by some of the ideas he has when writing.

The video was shot in Los Angeles by Anthony Mandler, and he cleverly had Rihanna and Ne-Yo sing in different places, as if they were lovers singing about how much they miss each other. Rihanna is in a hotel room and Ne-Yo is making his way there. As Ne-Yo is about to step out of the elevator, Rihanna steps into it; for a second they smile at one another. He then goes out and she continues down to the lobby. The twist is that they are each singing about different people. At the end of the video, Rihanna gets into her lover's car and Ne-Yo kisses his girlfriend in her hotel room.

'Don't Stop The Music' was the fourth single Rihanna released from her latest album, and it came out in September 2007. It was another of Rihanna's tracks that sampled a different artist's work, and this time it was Michael Jackson's 'Wanna Be Startin' Somethin''. It's not a profound song, though, it's just about having fun dancing at a club.

Both critics and fans loved how Rihanna introduced

house and techno to the track and it charted at No. 1 in Australia, Belgium, Austria, Hungary, Spain, Switzerland, Holland, Germany and France. It peaked at No. 3 in the US and No. 4 in the UK, and also performed well in other countries around the world.

Indeed, Rihanna's 'Don't Stop the Music' received many good reviews, with Tom Breihan from Pitchfork Media labelling it the best track in his view: '…an amazing bit of synth-bass Euroclub insanity; halfway through, sampled *mamasay-mamasas* from Michael Jackson's "Wanna Be Startin' Somethin'" come in and seamlessly blur into the track's overpowering beat.'

Nick Levine from Digital Spy agreed, telling his readers: '"Don't Stop The Music", the album's fourth single, finds Rihanna reaping the benefits of this beat-happy approach. A big, chunky floor-filler built around a looped sample of the "mama-se, mama-sa, mama-ku-sa's" from Michael Jackson's "Wanna Be Startin' Somethin'", it hands her an unmissable opportunity to sound sexy while wiggling her hips seductively. The whole thing works so brilliantly that, almost unwittingly, it's the best single to bear a "Jackson, M." writing credit since "Blood On The Dancefloor."'

The video was directed by Rihanna and TAJ Stansberry, and was the first video Rihanna had ever directed. They set it in an underground club that you can only access by walking through a sweet shop, and the majority of the video sees Rihanna and the other clubbers dancing. They filmed the day after the 'Shut Up and Drive' video shoot, in a club in Prague.

It was nominated for the 'Best Dancing Recording' Grammy in February 2008 but Justin Timberlake walked away with the prize for his video for 'Love Stoned'.

If Rihanna wasn't already busy enough promoting and recording her music, she also decided to do another tour, and this time it was on a much bigger scale than her 'Rihanna: Live in Concert Tour': she performed 80 dates in 30 different countries across the globe. It started in Vancouver, Canada on 15 September 2007 and ended in Mexico on 24 January 2009.

Her set list was mainly songs from her *Good Girl Gone Bad* album, although it also contained her favourite tracks from her first two albums. For the majority of her dates the set list was:

1. 'Pon de Replay'
2. 'Break It Off' (solo)
3. 'Let Me'
4. 'Rehab'
5. 'Breakin' Dishes'
6. 'Is This Love' (cover of Bob Marley's track)
7. 'Kisses Don't Lie'
8. 'Scratch'
9. 'S.O.S.'
10. 'Good Girl Gone Bad'
11. 'Hate That I Love You' (solo)
12. 'Unfaithful'
13. 'Sell Me Candy'
14. 'Don't Stop The Music'

15. 'Shut Up and Drive'
16. 'Umbrella'

For her European dates she added 'Push Up on Me' and 'Question Existing' and sometimes missed off 'Is This Love', 'Kisses Don't Lie' and 'Sell Me Candy'. Her set lists in Mexico, Asia and Oceania were different, because Chris Brown or Maria Jose would perform their own tracks first, and then Rihanna might perform the 'Cinderella' remix of 'Umbrella' with Chris during the show. She also introduced a medley containing 'Pon de Replay', 'Paper Planes' by M.I.A., 'Doo Wop (That Thing)' by Lauryn Hill and 'Live Your Life' (sung as a solo).

As well as Chris and Maria supporting her for some of her concerts, Rihanna had Akon or Kardinal Offishall with her for the Canadian dates. For some of the European dates she had Adam Tensta, and for the UK dates, she had David Jordan and Ciara. Kat DeLuna, DanceX and Ray Lavender also did some concerts.

RiRi must have consumed a lot of peppermint tea during her tour: if she has a hectic day and knows she'll be performing later, she drinks peppermint tea because it soothes her vocal cords. She loves performing for her fans, however, and enjoys it much more than performing at big awards shows.

This tour showed off how sexy Rihanna can be, and she wore several leather outfits which some people at the time thought were too revealing. She had totally changed her image from her first tour. Reviewers generally liked the show, and Jason Macneil from the Canadian Online Explorer wrote in his review of the Toronto show: 'The singer made a rather eye-popping impression, opening with "Pon de Replay" and clad in a sexy, dominatrix-like studded black leather ensemble.

'Supported by four dancers and a six-piece band, the performer did a bit of choreographed dance steps during the set but relied mainly on slick, radio-friendly hooks early on with "Let Me" from her 2005 debut album, *Music of the Sun*, and "Break It Off" from 2006's *A Girl Like Me*. The biggest highlight was the catchy, dance-infused "Don't Stop the Music" that had many boogieing in the aisles.'

Many reviewers felt that it wasn't the best concert they had ever seen, but for her first full-blown world tour, Rihanna did really well. MTV's Cheryl Leong said in her review: 'She succeeded in getting the audience in the entire stadium on its feet to an immensely enjoyable head-bobbing, feet-thumping, body-swaying fest. Taking a breather from her bouncy club hits, Rihanna brought on some of her slower tracks like "Hate That I Love You" and "Unfaithful."

'I did enjoy myself a whole lot at the concert. It just wasn't the most mind-blowing. Nevertheless, she did what she does best, which is to bring out an entire collection of #1 singles "live."'

For those fans unable to see the tour, Rihanna made it available to them via the internet, when she allowed MSN Music to host a recording of the Montreal concert on its site. A DVD was also made of the Manchester concert which was included on the deluxe version of *Good Girl Gone Bad: Reloaded.*

In April 2009 Rihanna would begin touring again, this time as a support act on Kanye West's 'Glow In The Dark' Tour.

A few weeks into 'The Good Girl Gone Bad Tour', she was spotted chatting to actor Josh Hartnett in the New York club, Pink Elephant. The press started saying they were an item, but this wasn't the case at all, as Rihanna explained in an interview with *Allure* magazine: 'This is what really happened. He and my management, they have each other's contact information. I went to Pink Elephant, and he came by. All of a sudden, the next day I'm seeing that we were kissing and hugging each other. You can't even go out with a friend who's a celebrity and have a good time without people making [bleep] up. Well, at least he's good-looking, right?'

Rihanna was so busy with the tour that she didn't have time for a boyfriend. She was jetting off all over the place, and having a relationship wasn't high on her priority list: when she had a day off, she just wanted to have a lie-in and then catch up on TV, not go on dates.

And she definitely didn't need the stress that relationships can sometimes cause. In one interview she talked about a former boyfriend to *Sugar* magazine: 'A few years ago I had a very insecure boyfriend. He kept breaking up with me for no reason, I'd cry all night and he'd just assume we would get back together the next day. Then I said "I'm not going through this anymore" and stopped returning his calls. It took ages to get over him, but that's when you need friends around you.'

Rihanna also had some advice for girls when it comes to dating: 'When guys move too fast, it's a sign they don't see you as special. Guys have tried to get frisky with me when we don't even know each other. Just get out of there!'

2008: RIHANNA, THE AMBASSADOR

In February 2008, Rihanna was appointed the Youth and Cultural Ambassador for Barbados. This was an amazing honour and privilege; the only person to have previously been given the title was the sprinter and Olympic medallist Obadele Thompson, after the 2000 Olympics.

During the presentation ceremony, the proclamation was read by Steve Blackett, the Minister of Culture: 'Whereas the Government and the people of Barbados truly acknowledge and celebrate the remarkable achievements of Robyn Rihanna Fenty; and whereas such an accomplishment has brought significant honour and deserving recognition not only to Rihanna but also to her beloved country and has elevated Barbados to the forefront of the entertainment world; and whereas this phenomenal success has come at so tender an age evoking invaluable inspiration and motivation to youth everywhere; and whereas all Barbados stands proud in the face of this honour and gives full support to Rihanna on her continuing path; be it now proclaimed in Bridgetown, Barbados that the Government of Barbados designates Robyn Rihanna Fenty an honorary Youth and Cultural Ambassador of this country.'

As well as the title, Rihanna also received a plot of land in June of the same year, so that she would always see Barbados as her home. The land was in the Apes Hill Golf Resort area, St James, and was worth $1.2 million (approx £727,000). In giving Rihanna such a valuable piece of land, the Minister of Housing and Lands, Michael Lashley, felt the government was showing how committed they were to people who promote Barbados in the wider world. There was one condition to the gift, though: if Rihanna decided to sell the land within 15 years, she would have to pay the government $100,000, as that was what they themselves had paid for the land. Some politicians disagreed with the attached condition and felt that the gift should have none: if Rihanna decided to sell it, then so be it.

Since becoming Youth and Cultural Ambassador for Barbados, Rihanna has helped to bring many thousands of tourists to visit the country who wouldn't necessarily have considered holidaying there, and she has considerably boosted the international profile of her home country by thanking the people of Barbados in various awards speeches and interviews.

Some Bajans (people who are native to Barbados) are jealous of her, though, and write negative things about the singer in blogs and on websites. They don't approve of some of the things Rihanna does, and want her to stop wearing such revealing clothes in her videos. Rihanna tries to avoid looking at these negative blogs, because reading hurtful comments upsets her too much. As far as she is concerned, she is comfortable with what she wears and that's all that matters. After all, she's not hurting anyone. If her mum had a problem with the way she dressed, most probably she would cover herself up, but Monica is fully supportive and proud that she is her daughter.

CURTAIN'S
FINALLY CLOSING

When Ne-Yo first wrote 'Take A Bow', Rihanna was overwhelmed, and she knew she had to be the one to record it. She wanted to create an anthem for women, and liked the idea of having a song which had the man as the cheater and the woman staying strong. Rihanna was able to draw on her own experiences, too: when she was a teenager, a boyfriend did the same to her.

'Take A Bow' was the first single to be released from *Good Girl Gone Bad: Reloaded* (it was also the fifth single overall from *Good Girl Gone Bad*). Released on 15 April 2008 in the US (and 12 May in the UK), it went straight to the top of the charts in many countries. It was No. 1 in the US, Canada, UK, Ireland, Denmark and Slovakia, No. 3 in Australia and reached No. 6 in Austria and Germany.

The video was filmed in Venice, Italy, and was again

directed by Anthony Mandler. It shows Rihanna's former boyfriend trying to apologise for cheating on her in the hope that she'll take him back. She won't accept his apology because she doesn't think he's sorry about cheating on her, just sorry she caught him. After staying in her house for a while (with him outside), she decides to drive off in her car but later returns and tells him to meet her there. When he arrives, she sets fire to some of his clothes (which are on the table) and leaves, not looking back.

Critics loved the track, and Chuck Taylor from *Billboard* magazine wrote in his review: 'With superstars Stargate and Ne-Yo at the helm, the velvety ballad ticks along with well-applied piano and strings, as the instantly recognizable singer delivers a convincingly bemused vocal, complete with haughty laugh.'

It was nominated for two awards at the MTV Video Music Awards 2008, Best Female Video and Best Direction. Sadly, it lost out both times, as the award for Best Female Video went to Britney Spears for 'Piece Of Me', and Best Direction was given to Erykah Badu for 'Honey'.

Rihanna collaborated with Maroon 5 on the track 'If I Never See Your Face Again', and this appeared on *Good Girl Gone Bad: Reloaded*. Maroon 5 had already recorded their own version of the song, which was included on their 2007 album, *It Won't Be Soon Before Long*, but they wanted to try something different with Rihanna. In fact, they liked her version so much that they released it as a single, rather than releasing their original version, and added it to the re-release version of their album, too.

The song was released on 26 May 2008 in the US and then a month later in the UK. It charted at No. 57 in the US charts and No. 28 in the UK. Worldwide, it did best in Australia and Holland, where it charted at No. 11.

The Rihanna version of 'If I Never See Your Face Again' is sung as a duel between a man and a woman. She was eager to be on the record because the band were friends of hers, she rated their music and liked the song. She told IGN: 'I've always been a fan of Maroon 5. I love the energy of the song and the lyrics are badass, so I was psyched to do it.

'[Filming the video] was fun, but it was difficult to get serious for the seductive scenes because Adam and I are friends. We would burst out laughing on every other shot – that was the best part.'

The video was directed by Anthony Mandler and they shot it in Castaic, Los Angeles. It was set completely indoors and the team wanted it to have an 80s glam feel. Throughout, Rihanna and Adam Levine flirt on a couch, bed and at a table but at the end of the video, Adam grabs her by the hair.

Fans of both Rihanna and Maroon 5 loved the video, and it was nominated for the Best Pop Collaboration with Vocals Grammy, but eventually lost out to Robert Plant and Alison Krauss's 'Rich Woman'.

'Disturbia' was the third single Rihanna released from *Good Girl Gone Bad: Reloaded,* and it came out in July 2008. It was written by Chris Brown, Andre Merritt, Brian Kennedy and Robert Allen, and was originally penned for a male voice. Rihanna was in the studio opposite when the guys were writing the song, and when she first heard it, she told them she wanted it. They never expected her to want to record a synthpop song: if she hadn't been there at that precise time, she might never have had the opportunity. Brown and Merritt recorded backing vocals for the track.

It topped the charts in the US, Belgium and New Zealand, reached No. 2 in Canada and Finland, and was No. 3 in the UK, Norway and France. Many critics felt that it was one of Rihanna's best songs ever, and it became the first of her tracks to go triple-platinum.

The song is about being frightened, and for the video, Rihanna and Anthony Mandler decided to set it in a torture chamber. They directed it together, and Rihanna wore white contact lenses to cover her irises and pupils in some scenes. She caresses a mannequin, she has tarantulas placed all over her body, and she gets tied up and chained up, too!

Yet again Rihanna was nominated for a Grammy but this time lost out to Daft Punk for their track 'Harder, Better, Faster, Stronger', which was named Best Dance Recording. She did win the award for Best International Song at the NRJ Music Awards in France, but when the Pussycat Dolls announced the winner, they said it was Katy Perry for 'I Kissed A Girl' instead. With 'Disturbia' playing in the background, poor Katy came on stage and gave a speech… only to find out later in the night that Rihanna was the real winner!

COUNTING
THE COST

Rihanna might have sold millions of records, but at this point in her career, she wasn't a millionaire by any stretch of the imagination. Like many singers in her position, she allowed others to sort out her finances and instead concentrated on making great records. According to the website blackarazzi.com, she fired her business manager, Patricia Williams, accusing her of stealing after she discovered how little there actually was in the bank.

Blackarazzi.com claimed Patricia Williams felt that she had to set the record straight. She said: 'It's not my fault that she only has $20,000 to her name. I have worked for many high-profile actors, musicians and multi-million dollar corporations. Why would I steal from Rihanna?

'I showed her all the paperwork and tried to explain the circumstances to her, but she wouldn't listen. She called me all sorts of horrible names and stormed off. I now feel compelled to share with the world the background story, as I will not allow my name to be slandered.

'Def Jam doesn't fund Rihanna properly, so Marc [her manager] uses the money Rihanna makes from third-party endorsements and from tours to fund her album and music videos.

'I don't want to disrespect Marc's name. He is a fantastic manager and genuinely believes in Rihanna, but he uses her money to fund her future projects because he believes he can break her in the world market. Her album sales are not nearly as close to her single sales and he knows that if she is only known as a "singles artist" she will only be as good as her last hit. Unfortunately, he didn't inform his client and I'm receiving the brunt of it.'

There was no official statement from Rihanna's management in response to either the article or the claims being made about how little RiRi actually had in the bank.

Rihanna collaborated with the rapper T.I. on his track 'Live Your Life', which was released in September 2008 in the US and November 2008 in the UK. It had been leaked online shortly before its release. Their track samples 'Dragostea din tei', by the band O-Zone.

Rihanna and T.I first performed it together on 7 September 2008, at the MTV Video Music Awards. It charted at No. 1 in the US, giving Rihanna her fifth USA No. 1 and T.I his third; it also made No. 1 in New Zealand,

No. 2 in the UK, No. 3 in Australia and Ireland, No. 4 in Canada and No. 5 in Austria and Holland.

The video was directed by Anthony Madler and plays backwards, with the start of the action being T.I battered and bloody at 6.33pm, and working backwards to 4.41pm to show what happened to him. Rihanna plays a singer, and the producer of the song, 'Just Blaze', makes a brief appearance as a man playing pool.

It won them a BET Award for 'Viewers Choice' and T.I also picked up the Best Male Video award at the MTV Video Music Awards. At the BET Hip Hop Awards, it scooped two awards: 'Best Hip Hop Collaboration' and 'Best Hip Hop Video'.

When Rihanna was invited by L.A Reid to sing on the 'Just Stand Up' record, she couldn't say no. She felt she had to be involved in the single, which raised money for the 'Stand Up To Cancer' charity, and joined forces with Beyoncé, Carrie Underwood, Sheryl Crow, Fergie, Leona Lewis, Keyshia Cole, Miley Cyrus, LeAnn Rimes, Natasha Bedingfield, Melissa Etheridge, Mary J. Blige, Ciara, Mariah Carey and Ashanti. Rihanna loves supporting charitable causes in whichever way she can.

Their single was released on 21 August 2008 and they also performed it on the 'Stand Up To Cancer' show, which aired on 5 September in the US. For the live performance, Nicole Scherzinger joined the group and sang Sheryl Crow's part, with the other girls covering for LeAnn Rimes and Melissa Etheridge, who were also missing. No video for the single was ever made, but it did well in the charts, reaching No. 11 in the US charts, No. 1 in the UK and No. 10 in Canada.

On 6 October 2008, Rihanna released the last single from her *Good Girl Gone Bad* album. 'Rehab' was released in the UK two months later. Charting at No. 18 in the US and No. 16 in the UK, it did better elsewhere: it was No. 3 in Holland, No. 4 in Germany and Norway, and No. 6 in Belgium.

Justin Timberlake and Timbaland wrote the track for Rihanna back in 2007. Timbaland went on to produce it alongside Hannon Lane, and Justin Timberlake appeared in the video as Rihanna's love interest. The track was actually one of Rihanna's favourites from the *Good Girl Gone Bad* album.

Rihanna explained how the track came about to EW.com: 'Well, Timbaland was on tour with Justin and we had to follow Timbaland, really. So we went to Chicago first and one night after the show, Justin just came into the studio and he started messing around, making a beat. And it was fun. We played around with that one, too. And when we came to New York, Justin came back to the studio and he was like, "I wanna write this song for Rihanna." So Timbaland had an idea and he knew he wanted to call the song "Rehab" and he had a beat. So then Justin Timberlake came in and he just put his thing on it. He wrote the song in his head, he didn't write anything on paper. He went into the booth and sang it, and I was very, very impressed. We all loved it.'

She went on to describe the track: '"Rehab" is a

metaphorical song. "Rehab" really just means, "we have to get over the guy". So we talk about checking ourselves into rehab, meaning we have to get over him. And we compare the guy to a disease or an addiction. We're just saying, "We don't wanna smoke any cigarettes no more," meaning we don't wanna deal with this (rubbish) anymore.'

They filmed the video at Vasquez Rocks Nature Area Park in California, and it was another video directed by Anthony Mandler. Some photos from the shoot were eventually leaked, and several websites suggested that Timberlake's girlfriend at the time (Jessica Biel) was jealous of the chemistry between Justin and Rihanna.

In the video Rihanna leans up against a vintage car in the middle of the desert. Justin arrives on a motorbike, then has an outdoor shower before approaching Rihanna. They get close a few times in the video, and Rihanna wears some gorgeous outfits while singing how he is like a drug to her. The video was a big hit and was awarded 'Best Music Video' at the Urban Music Awards, while Rihanna was named 'Best Female Artist'.

In the Digital Spy review, the journalist David Balls comments: 'The pop pair put in such a highly charged, effortlessly sexual display that it's no surprise Justin's lady was far from happy.'

Carol Han from fashion site StyleCaster commented: 'Rihanna's brand new music video for her single "Rehab" was just released today, and it literally left me breathless. The only thing that had me more mesmerized than the sight of

Justin Timberlake drenching himself in water, all scruffy-faced and hot, was the sight of Rihanna's amazing green bathing suit.'

2009:
THE ASSAULT

In the early hours of 8 February 2009, Rihanna's life changed forever. She had been enjoying herself at a pre-Grammy party held by Clive Davis, chief creative officer of Sony Music, and was on her way home with Chris Brown. According to the court documents that were filed months later, they got into an argument in the Hancock Park area of Los Angeles.

Rihanna had spotted a text from another woman on Chris's phone, and they got into a fight about it. Chris tried to force Rihanna out of the Lamborghini they were travelling in and repeatedly punched her in the face.

Hours later, Chris walked into LAPD's Wilshire station and turned himself in. Both cancelled their performances at the Grammys that night and their spots were filled by Nicole Kidman's husband Keith Urban and soul singer Al Green.

Chris would later release a video apologising for what he had done on his website and also apologised many times to Rihanna in private. Speaking on his behalf, his publicist said in a statement: 'Words cannot begin to express how sorry and saddened I am over what transpired. I am seeking the counselling of my pastor, my mother and other loved ones and I am committed, with God's help, to emerging a better person.

'Much of what has been speculated or reported on blogs and/or reported in the media is wrong.'

Her faith helped her through, and many people forget that she didn't just lose her boyfriend that night: she lost her best friend, too. She headed back to Barbados after the attack, but after three weeks she returned to Chris temporarily, before deciding to finish things with him permanently. During this time her whole family were concerned, with her mother telling *Star* magazine: 'I'm devastated, but what can I do? Rihanna is her own woman with her own mind and very, very independent. We love her but can't stand to see her play Russian roulette with her life. Chris has a bizarre power over her. She still loves him and he knows it. In her eyes, he's a god. Even after all this time, even after what he did, it is not diminished.'

Monica knows better than most what it's like to be in love and in an abusive relationship with a man who is physically violent. After all, it took great courage on her part to end her own marriage and raise the couple's three children on her own.

Rihanna's father also spoke to the press, and revealed to

People magazine how shocked and surprised he was when he heard the news. He also admitted that she was bruised, but she would get better in time and that he would end the relationship, if he was in her shoes.

Even though a couple of years have passed since that fateful night, Rihanna can't forget. She wishes now she had had the strength to walk away and not go back then, but she did go back to Chris for a time. She confided in *GQ*: 'It was a situation I always told myself I would never allow myself to be in. It's something I would force girlfriends to get out of. But there I was, sitting in it.

'I witnessed physical abuse happening to my mum and I always said I would never let that happen to me, and then it was happening to me. Now, when I look back at it, it just bugs me out that I couldn't see it for what it was.'

In the beginning she had wanted to keep what happened private, but once the press got involved, they wouldn't let it go without finding out every last detail. She would have done anything to stop the attack being leaked to the media, but there was nothing she could do but issue a statement. She told the magazine: 'Before that, I was just a little girl from the island, singing pop music. It was easy to think I was shallow and I had everything. It seemed like I had no problems in the world. And all of a sudden, boom! Everybody realises I do have problems.

'I have too much pride. I would rather put on a face. I would never let anyone see me cry. And I'm not like, "Please cry for me, I've been in a bad relationship". I hate that you know that and I don't want you to remember me for that.'

A few months after the attack the trial took place, and Chris ended up being sentenced to five years' probation and 180 days' community labour after pleading guilty to felony assault. While he was being sentenced, the judge told him: 'I am not immune to the chatter on the airwaves.' The press speculated that this might have meant that she knew that Rihanna and Chris were still communicating, or that it was a general warning because she watched television and listened to the radio.

Chris was to do his community labour at the Commonwealth Catholic Charities in Richmond, Virginia, and he also had to enrol on a 52-week violence counselling course. He was ordered to stay 100 yards away from Rihanna at all times unless they were at the same entertainment-related event, and then he must stay 10 yards away. The restraining order was to last five years.

In November 2009 Rihanna started to talk more openly about what happened to her. She confided in Diane Sawyer on *Good Morning America*: 'This happened to me, it can happen to anyone.' In the dark days that followed the attack, Rihanna found great comfort from God as he was there with her all the time, she admitted. She felt incredibly lonely at times, because she was the only person who knew what it had felt like to be in the car that night. Her mum and friends helped as much as they could, but it was hard for her because she still loved Chris despite what he had done to her.

Rihanna revealed that one night she decided to leave her house after a month of hiding indoors. She headed to a nightclub and danced – and started to feel alive again, after a month of being cut off from people.

Rihanna also talked about how going back to Chris afterwards was a huge mistake, and admitted that she now finds it humiliating to think that she did. She said: 'I stayed. I even went back after he beat me, which was wrong but again I'm a human being and people put me on a very unrealistic pedestal. And all these expectations, I'm not perfect.' She also admitted that he had bit her fingers and ear during the attack and had held her in a headlock.

Initially, she felt sorry for Chris after news of the attack broke, because he became so hated overnight – his own fans turned against him and no-one wanted anything to do with him. Rihanna loved him so much that she wanted to protect him, and that is one of the reasons why she went back. When she headed to Miami to be with Chris, she must have thought that things could get back to normal. They stayed at P. Diddy's home on Star Island, which is an exclusive artificial island with 35 homes (Will Smith, Madonna and Sylvester Stallone all own properties there). It should have been somewhere private, but the paparazzi wouldn't leave them alone. Chris was photographed on a jet ski with friends, but Rihanna stayed indoors most of the time and so no photos were taken of them together.

Once they decided to make another go of things, Rihanna's love for Chris soon turned to resentment. Everything about him started to annoy her, even though she pretended things were okay. Chris noticed the change in her and would ask her repeatedly whether she hated him, but she would always reply with a 'No'. Eventually she decided that she had to finish things for good: physically, her injuries might have healed, but emotionally, she was still hurting underneath.

When she heard Chris's YouTube apology, it felt as if he was reading from an autocue, as she explained to ABC News: 'I know that he felt really bad – I just didn't know if he understood the extent of what he did. The thing that men don't realise, when they hit a woman in the face – the broken arm, the black eye, it's going to heal. That's not the problem. It's the scar inside. You flashback, you remember it all the time. It comes back to you whether you like it or not, and it's painful. I don't think he understood that – they never do, they can't know that.'

Rihanna also worried that if she had stayed with Chris, other girls with physically abusive partners might follow her example and end up being killed. This was not something she was prepared to accept: she had to become a good role model and walk away. Chris might never have laid a finger on her again, but Rihanna was scared that the boyfriends of the other girls might have hurt them.

When the internet website TMZ published a leaked photo of Rihanna two weeks after the incident, showing all her facial injuries, she was more than upset. She told *Glamour* magazine: 'It was humiliating; that is not a photo you would show to anybody. I felt completely taken advantage of. I felt like people were making it into a fun topic on the Internet, and it's my life. I was disappointed, especially when I found out the photo was [supposedly leaked by] two women.'

In many ways she felt as if her life had been turned upside down overnight, and she also revealed to *Glamour*. 'I felt like I went to sleep as Rihanna and woke up as Britney Spears.' However, she was glad that she chose to do the interview with Diane Sawyer on *Good Morning America*, because of how it made her feel and the message it sent out to other young women. She told MTV: 'It was the biggest weight lifted off my chest. If you watch the interview, you see it was a subject that I didn't talk about for the eight months that I didn't talk about it, so that was my first real time opening up. I had a lot of tension bottled up. So when I finally spoke about it, it felt really good. More importantly, it felt good that people got something positive out of it, because it's devastating. It's not fun to talk about or listen to, but there are a lot of women who are going through it, a lot of teenagers who are scared to talk about it, so I thought it was a good thing that I can be that voice for them and help them get out of that situation.'

In another interview, she admitted that Chris had never hit her before that night but that he had shown signs of being controlling. She felt he was rather insecure at times and she revealed to *W* magazine: 'When people are insecure they become very controlling and they can get very aggressive and in turn abusive. It doesn't have to be physical. Like, they would say bad stuff to you to make you feel lesser than them just so they would have control in the relationship. It takes a big toll on your emotions and on your everyday life. It changes you.'

Ever since the incident occurred, interviewers have

constantly asked Rihanna about it, and even now, she still gets hassled. Rihanna would much rather talk about her new music and what she is doing at the moment rather than dwell on the past. She wants to be famous for her music, not for being the girl who was attacked – and she doesn't want to talk about Chris, which is completely understandable.

As well as God, her family and friends helping her to heal, music had a big part to play in her recovery too. She revealed to journalist Courtney Hazlett: 'I can tell you that making this album [*Rated R*] was my recovery. It's the way I vented and expressed myself.

'The minute I decided to leave the house again, I called up [Roc Nation President] Jay Brown and said, "I want to do music, I want to go back in the studio" – and we just did that. We started collecting songs and sounds, and putting producers together, figuring out who we want to work with to develop new sounds.'

DATING
AGAIN

Rihanna isn't a big premiere person, and so when she was spotted on the red carpet in London for the premiere of Brad Pitt's *Inglourious Basterds* in July 2009, the media started to ask why. They found out that she was there with Mr Hudson, an R&B singer on Kanye West's record label G.O.O.D. (Getting Out Our Dreams) and nine years her senior. They were on a date, but they didn't stand near each other on the red carpet: he was nonetheless there as her 'plus one'.

The *Mirror* reported that Rihanna met Mr Hudson (real name is Ben Hudson) while he was recording in the US, and afterwards the pair had kept in contact before arranging their date. Their source said the two had been meeting secretly, and once they got inside the cinema, they 'stuck together like glue.'

Afterwards it is thought that they went to the exclusive Mayfair restaurant Cipriani for something to eat, and then on to the movie premiere's afterparty at the Shoreditch House members' club.

When interviewed by BBC Radio 1Xtra the next week, Mr Hudson said: 'We just went to the pictures. She works hard, she's got to have something to look forward to at the end of the day.' He was then asked: 'Is there a relationship blooming?', to which he replied: 'No comment. I don't kiss and tell. I'm old fashioned, what can I say?'

And he was even asked about their date by the *New York Daily News*. He told them: 'We went to the movies. She's single, I'm single. I could say to a girl, "We're gonna do something this weekend," and at the last minute I'll be like, "Lil Wayne wants me to play trombone on his new track and I have to go do that."'

But the media were desperate for stories about Rihanna's love life and refused to leave her alone. She only had to be seen talking to a guy and they would be considered as dating. Only the week before the premiere, the press were saying that she was dating the rapper/producer Pharrell Williams! They claimed she was ringing him all time, going to his gigs and meeting up in the evenings while the pair were both in London.

The press also linked her to a man she used to date in Barbados when she was a teenager, after they were spotted on the beach together when she went home to see her family. Negus Sealy is three years older than RiRi and was photographed with her on the beach, holding on to her wrists and giving her a piggyback ride. He is supposed to have the nickname 'Love God', and the press suggested they were getting back together, although this was not the case: RiRi and Negus are just good friends now.

DANGEROUS
LOVE AFFAIR

Rihanna's first release of 2009, and also her first after the attack, was 'Run This Town' with Jay-Z and Kanye West. It was included on Jay-Z's album, *The Blueprint 3*, and was released on 11 August in the US (31 August in the UK). The song reached No. 2 in the US charts and No. 1 in the UK.

Rihanna, Jay-Z and Kanye won two Grammys for Best Rap/Sung Collaboration and Best Rap, and a People's Choice Award for 'Favourite Music Collaboration'. The critics gave very mixed reviews; some were extremely positive, some very negative and others were in the middle. One of the most positive reviews was by Pitchfork Media, who declared: 'There's something for everybody: Jay-Z sounds engaged in a way he rarely has since unretiring, Rihanna coos those "ay ay's" the radio loves, and Kanye

West, as you may have read, once again upstages the guy he's producing. Rihanna's hook may not be 'Auto-Tune'd, but it's definitely autopilot.'

The track samples the song 'Someday in Athens' by the 70s band, The 4 Levels of Existence. Jay-Z explained what it was about to DJ Time Westwood, simply saying: 'We basically run this town: it's myself, Rihanna and Kanye. It's pretty much it.'

The trio filmed the video in Fort Totten Park, New York. It was directed by Anthony Mandler and had lots of extras carrying fire torches and metal bars, with bandannas covering their mouths, listening to what their leaders were saying. There were explosions and during one section of the video, Jay-Z sings in a temple, guarded by members of the mob. The video ends with the three of them standing in an underground chamber.

Anthony Mandler explained to MTV how they came up with the concept of the video: 'There's a tone and feeling to the song, there's a militia, a march and a kind of rambunctious energy to it that, for me, I immediately wanted to tap into. I showed [Jay-Z] some references from the classic rebellious zones of the world. We live in a very orderly society in America, but when you get into Brazil, you get into the Middle East, you get into Africa, you get into Eastern Europe, when you get into places like that, there's a different sort of "we run this town" [going on]. There's less order and more chaos. So we looked at a lot of those references, new photos and historical photos, to capture that kind of falling-apart feeling.'

He added: 'We wanted you to feel uneasy throughout the piece, we wanted there to be a constant layer of tension through the piece. Even in the way I shot – where the camera comes by Jay, it doesn't stop on him, it goes to Rihanna – there's kind of this chaos of revealing and covering and concealing. And things happen off-screen that you don't see.'

SIMPLE
THINGS

Rihanna's life is so madly busy that she doesn't get to do some of the things the rest of us take for granted. If she wants to see a new movie that's being released, then she usually has to wait for it to come out on DVD, because she has hardly any free time, and if she went to a regular cinema she'd be mobbed by fans; movie premieres really aren't her thing either, so she wouldn't just go to one so she could watch a movie without being hassled.

Rihanna loves the movie *The Hangover* so much that she watches it again and again. She enjoys watching it with her friends or by herself, and she loves to scoff loads of ice cream or bags of Cheetos (cheese curl snacks).

The TV show she can't get enough of is *The First 48*, which is a documentary series about homicide and shows how detectives go about finding out who killed someone, collecting evidence, interviewing people and using hi-tech methods. The opening to the programme states: 'For homicide detectives, the clock starts ticking the moment they are called. Their chance of solving a case is cut in half if they don't get a lead within the first forty-eight hours.'

Rihanna finds the show really interesting, and will watch episodes back to back when she can. It is rare for her to be able to watch her favourite shows as soon as they air, because they are normally transmitted when she's on stage or at events: she has to either record them or buy the series DVDs when they are released.

THE WAIT
IS OVA

In October 2009, Rihanna's fans were treated to a gritty video less than a minute long in which she sang that the 'wait is ova.' The video was posted on her official website, and fans saw a new darker side to the star. The date 'Nov 23 09' was mentioned in the video and Rihanna tweeted: 'The Wait Is Ova. Nov 23 09' alongside a metallic 'R', but no one knew exactly what it meant. MTV tried to find out what was going to happen on 23 November, but Rihanna's representatives refused to give any answers. In the end they guessed that it was the date she was going to release a new album. And they were right: *Rated R* came out in the US on 23 November, although it was released a few days earlier in Australia, Germany and Poland.

For *Rated R*, Rihanna worked with Simon Henwood,

an artist, author and director. Henwood was given the job of reinventing Rihanna, helping to design the logo for *Rated R*, styling the music videos and making sure that the image projected of her was consistent with what they wanted it to be. He had been the creative director behind Kanye West's 'Glow In The Dark Tour' and had directed his video for 'Love Lockdown', which was nominated for three MTV Video Music Awards. Henwood first met Rihanna on Kanye's tour, and about a year later, they discussed ideas for *Rated R* when she was in London.

They worked together as a team, each coming up with ideas for how things should look. They also worked with other great designers and even visited Paris Fashion Week for inspiration. Rihanna was open to Henwood's ideas, but if she didn't like something, she would tell him.

He was the one of the main contributors to the book, *Rihanna: The Last Girl on Earth* (2010), which was a collection of behind-the-scenes photographs. The idea behind the book was that it would show the journey Rihanna made, from the first logo design to the world tour. Some of the photos show her on a rooftop, admiring the views in Paris; they also show her shoe collection and depict Rihanna posing with mannequins, escaping the paparazzi, enjoying room service and performing on stage.

Rihanna told MTV what fans should expect from the book, and why she decided to publish one: 'I think it was really special to have behind-the-scenes photos – you know, pictures that the fans haven't seen before all together of a very specific moment of my life, an album of my life. They just get to see all the things that they hadn't seen that were going on behind the scenes – really cool stuff, not typical. They're really fun photos. And even for me, when I look at them, they say so much. Photos really tell a thousand words.'

Her favourite photo in the book is one of her on stage wearing a headdress. The image has a green hue to it and Rihanna admits she calls it her 'Disturbia' photo.

The ideas Simon Henwood had as to how *Rated R* should be presented came from two main sources of inspiration. The first was a science fiction novel entitled *The Lathe of Heaven* by Ursula K. Le Guin. The plot centres round a character whose dreams have the power to change reality. His other inspiration was a 1971 movie called *The Omega Man*, which was based on the Richard Matheson novel, *I Am Legend*. Both the book and the movie gave him the idea of creating a world for Rihanna, a kind of dark dream that she could explore through her music. For the tour itself he wasn't afraid to show dark elements in the visuals, from burning naked mannequins and guns to broken glass and metal.

Rihanna confessed to the Daily Star: "Rated R in comparison to my previous albums is different... It's very honest, the sound is darker, I didn't want to make the same album I did last time.

"I pay attention to (the fans') comments, negative or positive. I want to keep them close with me and I want them to grow with me."

In starting work on her fourth album only weeks after the attack, Rihanna managed to turn something negative into something positive by letting her feelings about what happened influence her songwriting.

She revealed to MSNBC: 'It's a really fearless album – a lot of people are saying things like, it's dark, but it's a very honest album and I made it in a very truthful way. I let my guard down in telling my story and being a little more vulnerable and expressing myself. I really vented in my music. I go through a lot of different music and moods in the album. You definitely will learn a lot about what's going through my head.'

Rated R was released on 20 November 2009. Its tone was much angrier than her previous albums – *Music of the Sun*, *A Girl Like Me* and *Good Girl Gone Bad* – and more edgy. She wanted something different and allowed herself to change direction. The album reached No. 4 in the US charts, No. 2 in the UK and No. 1 in Switzerland and Norway.

Rihanna explained how she came up with the album's title, telling *W* magazine: 'It was really personal, it was from me in the most authentic way. It's like a movie, hence the title, in that when I was making this album – every day I was in a different mood. Sometimes I was pissed off, sometimes I was miserable, and every song brings out a different story.

'It's still hard to listen to certain songs, certain ones I couldn't even record. I'd keep pushing them back [on the schedule].'

One of the hardest tracks to record was 'The Last Song', because it's about saying goodbye to someone you love with all your heart. Rihanna confessed: 'When the label finally said we had 12 hours to turn in the album, I was like, "Okay, I have to do it." I just drank some red wine, dimmed the lights, got in the booth and sang it.'

Evan Rogers, who has been with Rihanna since the beginning, was at first shocked by the album and admitted to journalist Danielle Stein: 'This album was sort of like hearing your daughter using profanity for the first time. I'm not going to lie and say I didn't have concerns about how her core audience would react.'

Ne-Yo also saw a new side to the singer and admitted: 'When I first worked with her, on her second album, she was very – I don't want to say obedient, because it sounds like you're describing a dog – but she would take my suggestions without question.

'She trusted me, which was cool, but I told her that I ultimately wanted to get to a point where she would give me input, where she'd be a collaborator and not a puppet. And now I think we've gotten there. She's showing parts of herself that she didn't show before because she didn't want to scare anyone off. She's experienced some pain now, and it's helped her grow to a point where she's able to explore it.'

Because Rihanna's family are thousands of miles away in Barbados, she now has a second family made up of Jay-Z, L.A. Reid, Jay Bown, Tyran 'Ty-Ty' Smith, Melissa and her stylists. Carl Rogers and his wife consider Rihanna to be like a daughter to them and sometimes they want to protect her from certain situations.

Before *Rated R* came out, many fans believed that the

album's tracks would be all about Chris Brown and the couple's relationship, but this wasn't the case. As Chuck Harmony, one of the producers, explained to MTV: 'Whatever she came with, if she came out with "I still love you", that would have been about Chris Brown. If she came out with "I hate your dog", that would have been about Chris Brown, too. It's just a natural reaction for people to associate 'cause she's been so tight-lipped.'

Even if Rihanna had wanted to write songs about her former boyfriend, more than likely her songwriters would have refused. Ne-Yo confessed to Jayson Rodriguez: 'Chris Brown is a friend of mine and I don't view him as a bad guy for what happened. It was an absolute mistake and he has some lessons to learn and some maturing to do, but I'm not gonna bash him for that. I'm not gonna turn my back on a person I call my friend because he made a mistake. [So] I can't write the Chris Brown bash song and then turn around and look myself in the mirror.'

The album was recorded all over the world – in New York, London, Paris and Los Angeles. Rihanna's favourite tracks were 'Cold Case Love' and 'Fire Bomb'. She told *W* magazine: 'I wanted this album to have more bass, more bottom, grimier beats – to be less synth-y/pop-y/dance-y.

'My fans have until now been really young, like five years old to just before adulthood. But now older adults are into my music. Straight men, too! Men couldn't really bump my last album in the car. With this album they can play it and still feel tough.'

Critics generally liked *Rated R* and it was given a score of 76 out of 100 from Metacritic (which looked at 20 reviews to give its score); Jim DeRogatis from the *Chicago Sun-Times* gave it three out of four stars, and Ed Potton from *The Times* awarded it four out of five stars. In his review, Ed Potton said: 'By turns syrupy and strident, part lament, part tooled-up revenge fantasy, the best record Rihanna has made.' Jody Rosen from *Rolling Stone* agreed and declared it was 'one of the best pop records of the year.'

The tracks on the album were as follows:

1. 'Mad House'
2. 'Wait Your Turn'
3. 'Hard' (featuring Jeezy)
4. 'Stupid in Love'
5. 'Rockstar 101'
6. 'Russian Roulette'
7. 'Fire Bomb'
8. 'Rude Boy'
9. 'Photographs' (featuring will.i.am)
10. 'G4L'
11. 'Te Amo'
12. 'Cold Case Love'
13. 'The Last Song'

If you look at the covers of Rihanna's first three albums you will see a fresh-faced, happy girl showing her natural beauty, but for her fourth album, *Rated R*, she wanted something totally different. She was keen to reflect the change in her music and told *Elle* magazine: 'I wanted pictures that represented strength and fearlessness, but still femininity – a strong woman who can be vulnerable. Every woman is made up of vulnerability and strength – no matter what race you are, no matter what you've been through in your life. Every woman has that strength that is undeniable, but we also have really big hearts. It's just us.'

She commissioned fashion photographer Ellen von Unswerth to take some edgy portraits of herself and then RiRi picked her favourite for the album cover. Ellen von Unswerth is one of the best photographers in the fashion business, and she has shot the cover art for albums by Britney Spears (*Blackout*), Christina Aguilera (*Back to Basics*), Janet Jackson (*The Velvet Rope*) and Dido (*Life For Rent*).

The picture that Rihanna and her label liked best was one of her looking incredibly moody. It was a close-up shot, Rihanna's hand is covering up her right eye and she stares directly at the camera. One of her hands has several rings wrapped around her fingers, and she is wearing a leather outfit and dark make-up. It was shot in black and white, which made it seem almost aggressive, and they added in her 'R' logo in the top right-hand side corner. Many critics and bloggers noted how the *Rated R* cover was similar to singer Grace Jones' album covers. MTV commented in an article: '[The] grainy black-and-white cover shot that leaked Tuesday (October 27) finds the singer in a moody, contemplative pose reminiscent of outrageous 1980s avant-garde singer Grace Jones.'

The running theme in the cover art for the *Rated R* singles was that Rihanna was semi-naked. They were risqué, but tasteful at the same time. For the cover of 'Russian Roulette' she wore a gold corset that blended in with her skin tone to make it look as if she was naked. Wrapped around her body was barbed wire and on her right eye was an eye patch with the middle of it cut out so you could still see her eye. Her right arm points straight upwards, where a metal chain hangs. The title is written in a blood-red font with the extra-large 'R' logo over it: the sharpness of the point at the base of the 'R' makes it look as if it could slice into Rihanna's shoulder at any point.

MTV described the cover as controversial and the *Daily Mail* commented: 'Her daring outfits mean Rihanna is in the news as much for her fashion choices as her music, but the star has managed to combine the two on her new album cover.

'"Russian Roulette" sees the 21-year-old strip off, posing topless with nothing but a strip of wire wound around her chest to protect her modesty.'

For the 'Hard' cover she poses in a very revealing black bodysuit by designer Alexandre Vauthier, which only just covers her modesty. Her body is twisted towards the camera, her right elbow pointing upwards. Rihanna's eyes are shut and she is standing in a room with cassette design wallpaper. Again, it is shot in black and white, with the 'R' logo smaller than in the 'Russian Roulette' cover art and now in the top left-hand side corner. The single title is in red again, but appears like a stamp right across the middle of the cover.

Many fans and critics wondered what was going to come next, because with each single cover, she seemed to be removing more and more clothes.

For the 'Rude Boy' cover Rihanna was shown naked, but she used a large board with the single's title on it to hide her modesty. She wore a pair of masculine black boots, a top hat and in her mouth was a cigarette. Some people criticised her for 'glamorising smoking' on the cover but her fans felt she wasn't at all. She has smoked in several of her videos ('Disturbia', 'Wait Your Turn' and 'Rude Boy') but she isn't telling her fans to do so – it's just part of the character she is portraying in the videos.

Rihanna decided to go in a different direction with the cover art for 'Rockstar 101'. This was a much less aggressive cover, with her face being the main focus. Her hair is blonde apart from a black band at the front, which is covered in black netting. The eye make-up is still dark, with a patch drawn over her left eye but her lips are painted nude. She has one weapon-like earring on her left ear. The cover for the remix album was identical apart from the background changing to purple, which lifts the colour in her face.

For her international single 'Te Amo', Rihanna returned to her dark side and posed with a finger to her lips and her face touching a mannequin. It was a cover that screamed seduction and had the 'R' logo in the top left-hand corner.

The first single that Rihanna released from *Rated R* was 'Russian Roulette'. Released on 3 November 2009, it reached No. 9 in the US and Canada charts. It did better in Switzerland, Norway and Slovakia, where it topped the charts, and it made it to No. 2 in the UK.

Rihanna explained what the song was about to the Associated Press. She said: 'For me it was about being in a relationship and being afraid of getting hurt in the end, which is kind of the same feeling you go through playing the game of Russian roulette. You know that somebody could get hurt in the end and you're just terrified that it's going to be you. So when I said I'm terrified but I'm not leaving, then it means: I'm scared I'm gonna get hurt, but I'm in love so I'm not going to leave.'

Anthony Mandler was the director of the video, and he was the one who came up with the concept of having Rihanna imprisoned, interrogated, shot at underwater and run over, as well as having her play Russian roulette in the video with a gun. All in all, the video took two days to shoot. Before it came out, he confessed to journalist Jocelyn Vena: 'I think that with this song and the meaning of this song and how loaded it all is, no pun intended, how much imagery and perhaps symbolism that is loaded in this song, the only way to do it was to do something that was visually challenging.'

The scenes between Rihanna and her lover in the video were intentionally of secondary importance: 'I think our objective was to run down our lane with it and to step out of the drama and the gossip, to get deeper and be more symbolic.'

The video was up for the Best Female Video award at the 2010 MTV Japan Video Music Awards, but it was beaten by the Japanese R&B singer Namie Amuro's track 'New Look'.

WOMAN OF
THE YEAR

On 9 November 2009, Rihanna was honoured at *Glamour Magazine*'s Women of the Year Awards at Carnegie Hall, New York, alongside 11 other amazing women. She wore a gorgeous mermaid-style gown by the designer Stéphane Rolland that wasn't very practical, as she struggled to walk in it, but it looked amazing.

As her tribute video played, Rihanna couldn't help shedding a tear or two as she stood on stage. She told the audience: 'I couldn't possibly make it up here in this dress. As usual, I decided to wear the tightest dress I could find.'

She couldn't climb the stairs onto the stage because of the dress, and instead entered from backstage, not that anyone minded. Rihanna's award was presented by Iman, David Bowie's wife, who is a model, actress and successful businesswoman; Iman explained why Rihanna was picking up the Woman of the Year award by saying: 'This year we saw a different face of Rihanna – she's an indelible image of worldly pain and now, more than ever, I am more than impressed with her honesty and courage. She has taken her own scars and used them to create a new story of strength and awareness.' But Rihanna wasn't given the award just because of the way she handled herself after her attack, but because of what she had achieved musically, and for all the great work she had done for children's charities.

In her thank-you speech, Rihanna said: 'I am shaking right now, I am so nervous but I am overwhelmed and honoured over this honour to be *Glamour*'s Woman of the Year.' She also revealed that she had only just started thinking of herself as being a woman since she turned 21 and that she enjoyed being at an event to celebrate strong women. Her mum and her gran were her own 'Women of the Year', and she was so thankful to them, she continued. Indeed, she had flown in her family from Barbados so they could be at the event with her and help her celebrate.

It might have cost $50,000 to fly her mum, grandmother, brothers and aunts to New York, but it was worth every cent to Rihanna, as she loved introducing her family to Tyra Banks, Serena Williams and Stella McCartney after the awards ceremony. They then went on to the South Gate restaurant in the exclusive Essex House hotel for a meal together. She had been so busy promoting the album and

'Russian Roulette' that it was nice for Rihanna to just chill out and enjoy spending time with her family while they were in the US.

JUST
THE WAY

' Wait Your Turn' was originally going to be the second single that Rihanna released from *Rated R*, but her record label decided to release 'Hard' instead. Rihanna helped write this track with songwriters Tor Erik Hermansen, Mikkel S. Eriksen, Saul Milton, Takura Tendayi, Will Kennard and James Fauntleroy II. It was available to download from 13 November 2009, four days after the Woman of the Year ceremony.

A few seconds of the song were used in the promotional video for the album before it was released. Fans liked it and began downloading it in November once the album was available. It charted at No. 32 in Ireland, No. 45 in the UK and No. 82 in Australia.

The music video was shot in black and white by Anthony Mandler. It was filmed at night and has a Gothic feel to it, as Rihanna sings while walking down a street wearing an eye patch; she is also seen in a church and standing on a statue. Hip-hop videos of the 90s were the inspiration for the video.

TATTOOS

Rihanna has lots of tattoos, all over her body. On her neck she has 'rebelle fleur' (which means rebellious flower); she's also got a cascade of stars which run from the nape of her neck and go down her right shoulder. She had it done in two stages. Inside her left ear she has a tiny star and behind her right ear is the Pisces zodiac symbol. The Pisces symbol was done by a famous Brazilian tattooist who normally has a waiting list of three years, but he was able to do the tattoo for RiRi when they were both in Toyko.

On the top of her left shoulder she has her best friend Melissa's birth date in roman numerals: 'XI IV LXXXVI' (11 April 86), and on her right shoulder are the words 'Never a failure, always a lesson' written backwards. She has a small handgun on the right-hand side of her ribcage, which she says symbolises protection. Originally she had planned to have gun tattoos on both arms, but was unable to do so because she is the face of the make-up brand CoverGirl.

On the left-hand side of her ribcage she has 'Al Hurria fi Al Maseeh', which means 'Freedom in God' in Arabic. Down her right hip she wanted a Sanskrit prayer, which said 'Forgiveness, Honesty, Suppression and Control' but it was spelled incorrectly! Rihanna still likes it, though.

On her left ankle she has a skull and crossbones, with the skull wearing a red bow. She had this tattoo done in Miami. Currently she has three tattoos on her hands: the word 'Love' on the third finger of her left hand, a tribal pattern on her right hand and 'Shhh' on the index finger of her right hand (Lindsay Lohan and Lily Allen both got a 'Shhh' tattoo after Rihanna had hers done!).

Her tribal pattern tattoo was acquired while she was touring in New Zealand, and she opted for a Maori geometric design. At a UNICEF event in New York, she revealed to journalists from *People* magazine that it hurt a lot, but: 'It's tribal, it represents strength and love. It's their traditional way of tattooing – I always wanted [one].'

RiRi's favourite tattoo has to be either the gun on her ribcage, or her 'Never a failure, always a lesson' tattoo on her shoulder blade.

However, RiRi got in trouble when she decided to become a tattooist herself. She had been spending some time in her favourite tattoo parlour, the East Side Ink, with some friends and her bodyguard. She's had a lot of her tattoos done by the tattoo artist BangBang (real name Keith McCurdy) and when she has days off, she likes to go there and talk to him and the other tattooists who work there. He was the one who did her tattoo of Melissa's birth date, her gun, some of her stars and the 'Shhh' tattoo on her finger. After they had been there a few hours, in a big role reversal BangBang suggested she gave him a tattoo.

Rihanna agreed, because she loves tattoos and he's become a good friend to her over the years. He showed her what she needed to do, and she decided to draw him a little 'Umbrella', with the letter 'R' underneath on his leg. She did an amazing job, considering it was her first time.

After she'd finished she did two more tattoos on BangBang's colleagues. On Josh Lord's leg, she tattooed 'R 2' and on Patrick Conlon's arm, she tattooed 'R 3'. They posed for photos and after Rihanna left, she thought nothing more of it.

She had no idea that she had broken the law until the New York City Department of Health and Mental Hygiene announced they were investigating what happened. In a statement they said: 'Only licensed tattoo artists can administer tattoos in the city according to the City's Health Code. We are sending someone to follow up on this.'

Her ex-boyfriend Chris Brown is a big tattoo fan and he decided to follow RiRi's example a few weeks later, by tattooing BangBang himself. Both Chris and BangBang knew they would get in trouble because Chris didn't have a licence, and so they drove from New York to another state, where it was legal.

Chris decided to draw a cartoon face and wrote 'Bang' above it. BangBang thought that he did a better job than RiRi but when you compare the two tattoos, hers is by far the most tasteful. He has now decided that he wants more celebrities to tattoo him, and so he might be driving out of state quite regularly to get new inkings. At least Rihanna will be able to say she was the trendsetter and not a copycat!

Two months after Rihanna gave BangBang his tattoo, the New York City Department of Health and Mental Hygiene finished their investigation and the tattoo parlour was fined, though not for the Rihanna incident. A representative told MTV: 'Yes, a violation was issued to East Side Ink after an inspector found the parlour operating with an unlicensed tattoo artist on the site. All Health Code violations can range in fines between $200 and $2,000.

'Rihanna was not found at the parlour when the Health Department inspector followed up. The Health Department received a call about Rihanna, sent out an inspector; Rihanna was not at the site, the inspector conducted an inspection of the parlour and found an unlicensed tattoo artist operating on the premises – the Health Department issued a violation to the parlour for this unlicensed tattoo artist.'

In the run-up to Christmas 2009, RiRi had a new tattoo etched on the right-hand side of her collarbone, which reads 'Never a failure, always a lesson' backwards, so that when she looks in a mirror it is the right way round. The tattoo was done by BangBang, who revealed to OK! Weekly: 'She told me in advance she'd be coming, and then when she got there, she told me what she wanted: "Never a failure, always a lesson," but written backwards.

'I asked her why she wanted that and she said, "It's kind of my motto in life for everything. Instead of considering things to be mistakes, considering them lessons.'

She asked him to use grey ink rather than the standard black because it's a personal tattoo, rather than one she wants people to notice. As he explained: 'She wanted it to be more subtle, she didn't want it to draw too much attention.'

Rihanna is constantly getting new tattoos and confessed to *InStyle* magazine: 'My favourite thing is to be in New York, jump in a cab – on my own, no security – go to Sixth Avenue between Bleecker and Houston, and hang out in the tattoo parlours. It's a whole different culture.'

During an AOL interview, fans were invited to suggest questions they wanted Rihanna to answer, and Paul Beadle asked: 'Don't you think you'll regret all those tattoos when you're 70?'

But Rihanna didn't take offence and replied: 'Ask me when I am 70. I don't know but I don't think so. You think the gun might begin to sag when I get older? Well, I'll have to deal with that. They are personal messages to myself and they are meant forever. The tiny gun is indicative of power and protection. I did have a big one on my leg, but that wasn't a permanent one. It's not about violence. I have never used a weapon in a violent way and I don't intend to. What will my next tattoo be? A missile? No, it will be writing, I think. I'm really into writings. Someone was telling me about some writing on an Erykah Badu album sleeve called *Mama's Gun*. Its words and sayings are as powerful as a weapon. Maybe I'll have those next.'

CHRISTMAS AT HOME

Rihanna jetted home to Barbados to spend Christmas 2009 with her family. She might have seen them in November, but she still couldn't wait to catch up with them and find out what she'd missed. On her official website, she thanked her fans for supporting her throughout 2009 by writing: 'To all my fans, thank you for being amazingly supportive and loyal this year. Happy Holidays to you and your families.'

Rihanna spent Christmas Day on the beach with her family. She wore a stunning hot pink bikini, accessorised with a headband and large hoop earrings. The paparazzi will do anything to get photos of RiRi 24/7, even at Christmas. In the past they have even hidden in rocks in the middle of the ocean to get some shots of her; the first time Rihanna realised they had been there was when she saw the photos in an article. Seeing the images shocked her because she hadn't noticed the press, and from the angle they were taken she knew they must have been hiding in the rocks, quite far out from the beach.

After relaxing with her family on the beach for a few hours she changed into a black dress and went to a party at Kensington Oval cricket ground.

Rihanna was working on New Year's Eve and she flew to Abu Dhabi in the United Arab Emirates. She did a two-hour set on the lawns of the Emirates Palace Hotel in front of 10,000 fans, who each paid £66 to see the New Year in with her. After singing her biggest hits and ending with a rendition of 'Umbrella', she did the big countdown and celebrated with the audience and her friend, baseball player Matt Kemp, who had come along to support her. He was to become her boyfriend in the weeks that followed. The party continued until the early hours in a huge tent.

The organiser of the event, John Lickrish, told the press: 'Tonight was a huge success and a truly memorable way to end a great year for Flash [Entertainment] and Abu Dhabi. Rihanna's performance left us all breathless and set a very high benchmark for next year.'

Rihanna must have been excited to see what 2010 would bring, after the troubles she had had in 2009. She set herself a huge list of New Year's resolutions: she wanted to start getting up early, stop being late for things, cut down on her shopping trips, learn to play the drums and see more of her mum and family. Musically, she wanted to work with Depeche Mode. She chatted to Nova FM about her dream collaboration: 'I wanna work with Depeche Mode or The Prodigy – I really love their style. I love the new Prodigy album, they really inspired me with their style. I really got into the dubstep and that whole underground sound, the grimy sound and aggressive lyrics; I was really glad to hear that.'

Sadly, she hasn't had her wish to work with Depeche Mode or The Prodigy granted yet, but you never know. When Rihanna wants something, she generally gets it!

2010:
INTRODUCING MATT

The news that Rihanna was dating baseball star Matt Kemp broke in the first week of January 2010. After her New Year's Eve performance they travelled to Mexico for a holiday, where the paparazzi managed to get shots of the pair relaxing in a hot tub together. They also snapped Matt with his hand on Rihanna's backside and the two of them kissing. Rihanna had lots of fun on the holiday and got the opportunity to swim with dolphins. However, it wasn't a romantic vacation with just the two of them, because she brought along her friends. They hung out as a group, went to the Beach Club, El Squid nightclub in Cabo San Lucas, enjoyed a yacht cruise and had fun on jet skis.

While the couple were on holiday, Matt's agent was asked by E! Online whether they were dating. He denied everything, saying: 'I think dating might be a stretch at this point. They are in Cabo, but past that they are just good friends and I don't think we can label it as anything other than friendship right now. Who knows what will develop past the friendship.'

Rihanna tries to keep her relationships private but the press never let her. They always rush things, which must frustrate RiRi at times.

FACT FILE – MATT KEMP

Three years older than Rihanna, Matt Kemp plays for the Major League Baseball team, the Los Angeles Dodgers. His position is outfielder, and baseball is his life. Growing up in Oklahoma, he always excelled at baseball and basketball in school.

Most of his friends are baseball players, and Rihanna was his first celebrity girlfriend. His nickname is 'The Bison', because a commentator called Don Sutton once said during a game that he looked 'like a big buffalo running around the bases.'

It must have been nice for Rihanna to date someone who wasn't involved in the music scene, but who at the same time knew how to handle fame and fans. Like Rihanna, charity work means a lot to Matt, too.

He also shares her love of tattoos and he has quite a lot of them himself: he has a tattoo sleeve on his left arm, which has a Greek mythological figure with a sword; a rose; a script text on his chest; and 'Living For The Moment' across his back.

After returning home, Rihanna decided she needed some new bikinis, and asked Celeste Johnny to design her some especially for her. On her official website, Celeste states: 'Johnny Vincent [her swimwear company] was born out of my love for fashion and the Caribbean, in essence my 'Paradise'. It is my goal that through my designs, fabric, colours and accessories you will feel just that. I hope the passion that I create with is shown in my designs and transferred to you when wearing my pieces. I am a true believer in loving oneself, loving the beauty that is unique to us all. I truly hope you will feel how beautiful, wonderful and sexy you are when you wear one of my designs. I hope you truly feel the love of my paradise as it embraces you.'

Rihanna loves Celeste's bikinis, and was photographed wearing a hot pink design at Christmas and on her holiday. Fans rushed to the site to order them for themselves and they soon sold out.

Celeste was thrilled when she was asked to design a bikini especially for Rihanna and told *OK! Magazine*: 'She looked great and I just got an email that she wants a striped bikini, so I'm kinda going over things with her assistant as far as, like, the colours that she wants.'

Rihanna has become a fashion icon, and millions of women around the world would give anything to look like her. She can take any item of clothing and use it to make a statement. Her clothes reflect her personality, and you can often tell how she is feeling by what she is wearing.

After her holiday, RiRi had to get straight back into her

work because she had singles to promote. The second single to be released in the US from *Rated R* was 'Hard', featuring the rapper Young Jeezy. It was released on 19 January 2010 in the US and in August 2010 in the UK.

The track was written by Rihanna, Young Jeezy, and Tricky Stewart and The-Dream. 'Hard' reached No. 8 in the US charts and No. 42 in the UK. The track wasn't given a worldwide release, but fans from other countries did download it and it charted at No. 9 in Canada, No. 15 in New Zealand, No. 21 in Slovakia and No. 26 in Sweden.

Both fans and critics loved Rihanna's vocals on this track and its hip-hop style. The video was directed by Melina Matsoukas, who came up with the concept of basing it on a military operation in the desert. The clothes Rihanna wore made a statement, and it was clear that she had fun shooting it. She admitted to MTV: 'It's couture-military. Everything is surrounded by the whole idea of something military. We have tanks, we have troops, we've got helicopters, we've got explosions… Tight gear, lots of cute outfits, lots of bullets. Crazy.'

She also talked about what she loves about 'Hard': 'When I first heard the song, I was in Paris. Dream and Tricky, they flew out and played me the record. They played me a few [songs], but this one stuck out to me. It had such an arrogance to it, which is so far from who I am, which is part of why I wanted to do it. It was fun, it was bragging – a lot of attitude. Young Jeezy was the perfect person for the topic of the song, just the vibe of the song. I love, love, love his verse. He added so much more to the record.'

The song went on to win the Viewer's Choice Award at the 2010 Bet Awards.

After the Haiti earthquake hit on 12 January 2010, Rihanna was deeply affected; when she was interviewed on a Norwegian talk show she explained that it felt to her as if the earthquake had hit Barbados. She said: 'In the Caribbean, we think of ourselves as one big family, one country... we're all together. We all represent each other.'

Rihanna wanted to do something personally to help. She decided to release her own version of the Bob Marley Classic 'Redemption Song' and released it for download on 19 January, a week after the earthquake struck. The money she raised was given to the Help For Haiti appeal.

It was only available to download for 48 hours and charted at No. 18 in the US charts, thanks to an appearance on *The Oprah Winfrey Show* the day after its release. Rihanna had performed the song and also spoke about why she was releasing it. She told Oprah and the audience watching at home: 'This song for me, growing up, anytime there was a difficult situation, I always listened to this song because it was so liberating. Even now I listen to it when my back is up against the wall. I feel like the people of Haiti need to hear something inspiring.'

She later added: 'Often in a tragedy like this, it's the orphans who suffer most. In Haiti, they've already had almost 400,000 orphans prior to this. There are so many kids out there without parents, who can't find their parents. There are a lot of kids dead, a lot of kids hungry, they have no way to get food, they're helpless. That's why we have to take care of them: the children are the future.'

Rihanna also sang on another track to raise money for the people of Haiti. 'Stranded (Haiti Mon Amour)' was sung by Rihanna, Jay-Z, Bono and The Edge (from U2). This track was released on 23 January 2010.

The song was written as a direct response to what had happened. Producer Swizz Beatz texted Jay-Z and Bono to see if they wanted to do a single, and both agreed. Bono actually came up with the song's hook while talking to Swizz on the phone.

Swizz revealed all to *Rolling Stone* magazine: 'The idea of the song is "We're not gonna leave you stranded" and that's what the chorus is, so me and Bono started going back and forth with ideas, and he was like, "You know this word stranded keeps standing out to me…" and I asked him to sing it, and he put me on hold 'cause he's recording the ideas on a Dictaphone – so he did it there and then on the phone.'

They all spent about three hours on the phone talking about the song and then the Edge worked on what they had come up with after they recorded it separately. Rihanna was then brought in. Swizz explained: 'I knew that Jay would be able to tell a story, and that Bono would be able to sing and bring it home. The last component that I added was Rihanna, and she's kinda like the angel that's on the track, softening it up and giving it that caring feeling, because this hook is so powerful.'

It was performed live at the London leg of the 'Hope for

Haiti Now:A Global Benefit for Earthquake Relief' telethon, which was hosted by *Twilight* star Robert Pattinson. Other stars gathered in Los Angeles and New York as this was where the rest of the telethon took place. George Clooney hosted the Los Angeles leg, while Wyclef Jean ran proceedings in New York.

The track charted at No. 16 in the US, No. 41 in the UK, No. 3 in Ireland, No. 10 in Austria, No. 14 in Denmark and No. 39 in Belgium. Money raised from the single and the telethon went to several charities including Oxfam America, UNICEF and Partners in Health.

On 27 January 2010 a very special girl called Jasmina lost her fight against leukaemia and died. Rihanna was very close to Jasmina, and her death affected her deeply. She had been one of the celebrities who launched a campaign to find the little girl a bone marrow donor. Rihanna had loved her energy and the fact that she was always smiling.

When the news of her death broke, Rihanna released a statement. In it she said: 'I am incredibly heartbroken that Jasmina has passed away. She was such a brave and special child.

'She showed me more strength and spirit than many adults I have met. I feel blessed that I was able to have her in my life, and know that through her example, she has saved many lives. She was truly an angel on earth.'

Jasmina touched the lives of many people, even President Obama. He too released a statement, in which he said: 'It is with great sadness today that Michelle and I extend our condolences on the passing of Jasmina Anema.

'Jasmina showed tremendous bravery in the face of adversity, and her ability to stay positive throughout her battle was an inspiration to me and to all those she touched.

'As the parents of two young girls, our hearts particularly go out to Jasmina's devoted mother Thea. Our thoughts and prayers are with her and with all who knew and loved Jasmina.'

A month later Rihanna decided to do more to help those fighting leukaemia. She wanted to raise funds for DKMS, which is the world's largest bone marrow donor centre, and so she asked the Pepsi Refresh Project to donate $25,000. Pepsi were already giving away a total of $20 million, and the public had to put forward worthy causes and charities that they felt deserved a cash injection. Rihanna and DKMS' aims were to: 'Raise awareness of the impact of blood cancers such as leukaemia, aid the 10,000 people in need of a bone marrow transplant each year, help the 70 per cent of patients who rely on strangers for a second chance, and recruit and register nearly 4,000 new bone marrow donors.'

Rihanna hosted the kick-off party for the project on 5 February 2010 at the LIV Nightclub, Miami Beach. Her project got the funding it needed after she secured enough votes. The idea behind the Pepsi Refresh Project is that people are invited to come up with an idea, promote it, people vote and then if it gets enough votes, Pepsi gives the funding.

Rihanna will always use her fame to help people, and

will continue to speak for people who need transplants. She will never give up, because she wants to help save people's lives.

Having started the year with two charity singles, 'Rude Boy' was Rihanna's first single from *Rated R* to be released in 2010. This was another track that she had co-written with Stargate, Ester Dean, Makeba Riddick and Rob Swire and it came out on 19 February.

This track used dancehall and ska elements, and both fans and critics loved it. The song became the bestselling single of *Rated R* in the US and entered at the top of the charts for five weeks. It was also No. 1 in Australia and Bulgaria, No. 2 in the UK and Slovakia and No. 3 in Ireland, New Zealand, Norway, Denmark, Belgium and Hungary.

The video was directed by Melina Matsoukas, who had previously directed 'Hard', but this time, she wanted 'Rude Boy' to have a Jamaican dancehall vibe and she certainly achieved it. It was the first of Rihanna's videos to be shot in front of a green screen, which allowed the graphics to be added later. When she's dancing on top of the zebra and the lion, Rihanna had to use her imagination to try and picture what the finished video would look like. She also got to show off her dancing skills as she picked out iconic dancehall moves from the 90s, such as the 'Butterfly' and the 'Bogle' dance.

The video shoot took place in Hollywood, Los Angeles, and Rihanna found it a lot of fun to film, because it wasn't as dark as some of her previous videos. She really liked the concept, and told MTV in an interview: 'It's really colourful; it's a pop art video.

'We shot it all on green screen. Everything was done in post-production. It's really colourful, really energetic. It was really inspired by my Caribbean roots. I love reggae music. [Rude Boy] is a Jamaican term, so our costumes are dancehall-queen-like. It's a fun video, probably the most fun video we've done so far.'

One of the writers behind 'Rude Boy', Makeba Riddick, revealed how the song came about to *Us* magazine. She said: 'Rihanna and I both work with Stargate a lot – the production duo from Norway – and they had the track and started the idea with another writer, Esther Dean. She actually came up with that concept, but the song wasn't done and there were things Rihanna wanted to change, so they brought it to me to finish. I was listening to the words and me and Ri, we were just laughing and talking about so many situations that have happened in the past and that happen to women everywhere. By the time we were done of course, we were laughing and giggling about the lyrics – surprisingly everybody went nuts over the song.'

Makeba was very surprised when 'Rude Boy' got to No. 1, and only found out when people started tweeting her to say congratulations. One minute, the track had been at No. 4, and the next it was at No. 1. Rihanna was even more excited, because she had written most of the lyrics for the track, and she felt it was the strongest one of the album.

'Rude Boy' was nominated for 'Best Editing' in a Video

award at the 2010 MTV Video Music Awards, but was beaten by Lady Gaga's 'Bad Romance', which was directed by Jarrett Fijal.

HAPPY BIRTHDAY, RIHANNA!

Rihanna turned 22 on 20 February 2010, but she actually celebrated five days earlier in Australia. She was there to promote *Rated R,* and *WHO* magazine decided to throw her a massive party. They invited 200 people, from *Home and Away* stars Luke Jacobz, Tessa James and Esther Anderson, to Jermaine Jackson and *So You Think You Can Dance* winner Talia Fowler. She was given a gorgeous zebra-print cake with star sparkles.

The guests enjoyed the exquisite canapés on offer, but Rihanna decided to give them a miss because she was going for an Italian meal once the party was over. She looked stunning in a nude minidress by the designer Boudoir D'Huitres, and told journalists from *WHO* that her favourite Australian designers were Sass & Bide (Sarah-

Jane Clarke and Heidi Middleton). During her three days in Australia, she also wore Sass & Bide jeans.

She was glad she saved herself for the meal, because she found the cuisine at Beppi's Italian Restaurant 'hands down the best food in Australia.' She wasn't the first celebrity to rate Giuseppe Polese's talents, though: Pink had dined there the previous August and wrote in their visitor's book that they needed to move to LA. They sent her a cookery book with their recipes in it, and she started cooking from it. However, Pink and Rihanna aren't the only famous diners Beppi's has entertained: over the years they have fed Frank Sinatra, astronaut Neil Armstrong and *Pirates of the Caribbean* star Geoffrey Rush.

While in Australia, Rihanna also spent time at the Sydney Aquarium, and went on a cruise around Sydney Harbour.

When she returned home, Matt threw her a big birthday party in Phoenix on the Saturday. She had known he was planning something, but expected it to be just the two of them and her closest friends. He had employed a Jamaican chef to do the food, and there were scrumptious cupcakes to tuck into. It is thought that it took him a whole month to plan everything and make sure it was perfect for RiRi. Some of his Phoenix Suns buddies came along, too.

Rihanna's birthday cake was extremely personal to her as it had all her tattoo designs on it, and she looked happy and relaxed as she danced the night away, wearing a toy crown. The evening before, they had been out with their friends to the Revolver nightclub, and after the festivities of Saturday, they relaxed and enjoyed a low-key brunch with her friends.

It is thought that Matt bought her a diamond necklace, but there has been no official confirmation.

The whole weekend was a chance for Rihanna to let her hair down and relax. It was completely different from her 21st birthday the year before, which was shortly after she was attacked. Her record company cancelled the party they were planning for her, and instead she went to the cinema with just a few friends. The next day she travelled to Mexico and had an amazing time, although it seems she got so drunk she can't remember everything.

Rihanna confessed *I-D*: 'The most drunk I've ever been, my friends could probably tell you better because I blacked out. But it was in Mexico, on my 21st birthday. We went off to this island by boat – it's so secluded, like you can't drive on it, so there's no cars, no schools, you take a boat to and from. But there's a village on the island and the locals, the natives, they made me moonshine [home distilled alcohol]. Straight out of the tub, they made it and brought it to me in an empty water bottle.

'I'd been hearing about moonshine, "It's like the worst, it will kill you!" I'm like, "Okay, let me take a shot of this ever-so-tough moonshine." I took a shot – nothing. I was so disappointed. Took another shot – nothing. Eight shots later – still nothing! An hour later, I got out of the boat, got into my car, got back to my house, got into the pool, played volleyball – in the pool! And then I can't remember getting out of the pool. I woke up in different clothes. Different

Left: Rihanna begins her journey to superstardom, performing in New York in 2005.

Below: She auditioned for Jay Z's Def Jam Recordings when she was 16 and was snapped up immediately by the hip-hop star.

Rihanna is a worldwide music star and international style icon.

Above: Rihanna remains close with her father Ronald and regularly returns to visit him in Barbados.

Left: Rihanna holds aloft her award at the 50th Grammy Awards ceremony in 2008.

Rihanna shoots the video for 'Rehab' alongside Justin Timberlake in 2008.

Rihanna had a rocky relationship with former boyfriend and singer Chris Brown. She appeared on stage with him at the Jingle Star Ball in 2008 (*above*), only a few months before Brown was in court on charge of assault against Rihanna (*left*).

Apart from her music career, Rihanna is also a 'style' and 'fashion' icon...

Above: Rihanna performs alongside Kanye West on the Jay Leno Show in 2009.

Below: Rihanna celebrates New Year's Eve with Kanye and mentor Jay Z in Las Vegas in 2010.

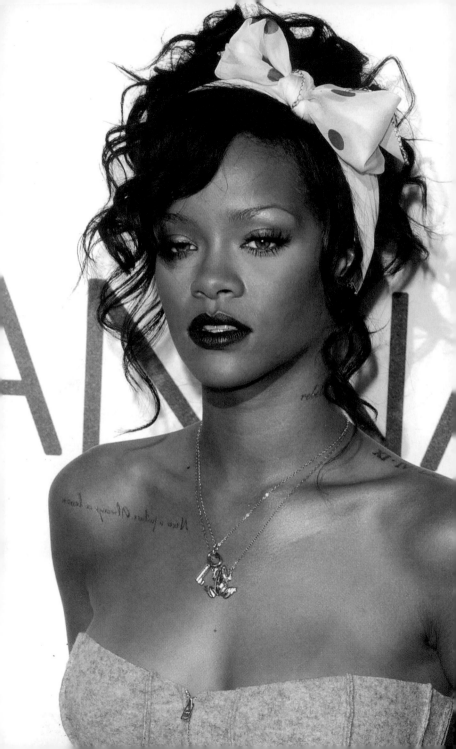

underwear. Like different underwear? And how did I get in my bed?'

She also revealed what her favourite tipple is: 'I like Jameson and ginger. Actually, dark liquor is the only one that doesn't give me a hangover. I don't always get a hangover, but if I do get a hangover, it's with vodka.'

. Some of her closest friends left 22nd birthday messages for Rihanna on her official fansite.

Singer Shontelle, her friend and former drill sergeant, wrote: '22 is all that more special a number because that's how many years the world has been blessed since the day you were born. I'm really proud of you Rock Star! You run this town. Keep it coming harder! Stay beautiful inside and out. Happy Birthday Robyn!'

Evan Rogers and Carl Sturken, who discovered the star, wrote: 'It seems like just yesterday that we celebrated your 17th birthday and getting a record deal almost at the same time …you've come so far and grown so much, we couldn't be anymore proud of you…. HAPPY B-DAY!!!'

Fellow Bajan performer Hal Linton added: 'Happy happy Birthday Rih! Sending my blessings and all that good stuff, wishing you many more.'

Rihanna also got thousands of messages from fans. They sent her cards, presents and special scrapbooks they had made.

FASHION

Rihanna loves fashion, and when she was growing up, her style icons were Mariah Carey, Madonna and Marilyn Monroe. She always wants to make a statement with what she wears in her videos, at award shows, events… even when she's out shopping. The singer likes her clothes to be an extension of her personality and of how she is feeling, rather than just costumes designed to shock or generate column inches in newspapers. Altogether, she has 1,500 pairs of shoes in her closet to choose from, so she never has any excuse for not wearing matching shoes!

Rihanna admitted to *InStyle* magazine: 'I've been a fashion fanatic since I was little, looking at all the international magazines, but I used to dress like a boy when I was a kid. I'd wear my brother's baggy pants and his sneakers. Now I like little skull caps, jeans, flat boots that come up to the knees. And then I play around with the top – a big T-shirt or a sleek camisole, or a jacket. I love jackets! I have a million.'

Being fond of daring accessories can sometimes cause problems, though. She told the *Daily Telegraph*: 'At Fashion's Big Night Out, I wore this spiked bracelet. I saw so many people I knew and everyone I hugged was flinching. It took [hugging] four people before I realised what was happening. And then my earring started to stab me on my shoulder. That was dangerous!'

Rihanna did look fabulous that night, as she wore a black cowl minidress by Alexander Wang and some studded sunglasses, which went well with the bracelet.

She divulged to SugarScape: 'With fashion, the simplest thing like a star or a flower can inspire you. I'm into a lot of stuff to do with nature and colours now, just things that are really expressive.

'I wear a lot of Stella McCartney because what she does is great – she's a top, top designer.'

RiRi talked to *Elle* magazine about other fashion designers she admires. She confessed: 'It's clear there are definitely fewer black women in the high-fashion industry. One of the things I respected most about Gucci was that they did a print campaign with me. I'm a black girl on a fashion spread for Gucci – that was a big deal. I respect designers who aren't afraid to go outside the box. I went to a Jean Paul Gaultier show, and I saw girls who are thicker than me, beautiful and voluptuous and different ethnicities. That made me so excited. I thought, Okay, I can work that, for sure.'

RiRi thinks Victoria Beckham is very stylish and told the *Sun*: 'I love Victoria Beckham's line, it's so feminine and chic.' She admires the effort the designer puts in to create her dresses, accessories and trousers, adding: 'Really sexy, really, really tailored. That's what she is. She's put a lot of effort into it.'

Our favourite singer has always been a risk-taker when it comes to fashion. She likes choosing unusual items when she's out shopping and using them to create a unique look. When it comes to dresses, she likes them to stop at the knee and show off her curves; she also likes minidresses with long sleeves. She isn't the kind of celebrity who only wears an outfit once either, as she likes to get her money's worth. The favourite items in her wardrobe tend to be jackets, because they can completely transform an outfit and make it look completely different.

When it comes to shoes, she likes ankle boots and sneakers, and she likes tomboy-ish jeans, as she explained to *Seventeen* magazine: 'For everyday, I like jeans that are supposed to be skinny jeans but aren't tight. I like them tomboy-ish so that they're almost a size or two bigger than my normal size and slouch a bit. When I go out, I like a more structured jean because, for my body, they're more flattering on my legs.

'I love sneakers and my favourite sneaker is the Nike Blazer. I don't really like low-tops, but if a high top is paired with skinny jeans, it makes your feet look really big, but the Blazer gives a really good shape for girls, especially with skinny jeans.'

It might seem as if Rihanna looks glam all the time, but when she's on her tour bus, it's comfort that matters most to her: she ditches her heels for sneakers and wears sweatpants and pyjamas. In fact, she travels relatively light, as all her stage clothes are looked after by other people in her team.

MEETING THE PARENTS

Things went up a notch between Rihanna and boyfriend Matt Kemp in March 2010, when RiRi met his family. She had been performing at the Echo Awards in Germany, but decided to fly all the way to Arizona to support Matt, who was hosting a special event called 'Ante Up for Autism' to raise money for the charity TACA (Talk About Curing Autism). The charity's motto is: 'Families of autism helping families with autism'. The night had a casino theme and they enjoyed dinner, dancing and cocktails.

It would have been easy for Rihanna to miss the event because her schedule is so packed, but she wanted to be there for Matt. His brother is autistic, so he wanted to help raise as much money as possible. He got his wish, as $170,000 was donated, which is approximately £104,000. That is an amazing amount of money, considering there were only 150 people at the event. Rihanna also got the chance to meet Matt's family, before starting her 'Last Girl on Earth Tour'.

The tour was due to start a few weeks later, and Rihanna was well into preparations: she wanted to make sure that her concert would be the best concert her fans had ever seen, so that meant long hours of rehearsal. In the midst of these preparations, she was invited to appear on *American Idol*, an opportunity not to be missed.

Most acts would be nervous performing on the *American Idol* stage, with 20 million people watching at home, but Rihanna seemed to take it in her stride. Indeed, she had been so busy that she hadn't been able to rehearse a special routine, so she had to make it up on stage during the limited rehearsal time. She decided to perform 'Rockstar 101', which was due to be released in May 2010, and wore a black skin-tight catsuit, which perfectly suited the song.

Rihanna felt comfortable enough to admit to *American Idol* host Ryan Seacrest that she was dating Matt, but tried to imply it wasn't a big deal. She said: 'He is my boyfriend and yeah, it's new and fun. It's nothing too serious. I don't want anything that's going to take up so much of my energy and time in a bad way. I just wanna have fun, and that's what it's about.'

But she wasn't the only one having to put in the hours to prepare for the tour – her whole background staff and crew were working flat out, too. Stylist Mariel Haenn was one of about 30 people putting together the different looks Rihanna and her dancers would have. They had to create mood boards, collect interesting fabrics they thought would look good, and sketch outfit ideas for Rihanna and her inner circle to look at and decide what they liked (and what they didn't). The outfits had to compliment the different tracks Rihanna would be performing and be easy to remove for the quick costume changes.

Mariel explained what work was involved to thisismax.net, shortly before the tour started. She said: 'Rihanna, band, dancers, and background vocalists all to be dressed with specific creatives and looks that are thought out thoroughly and all determined by the music. 5 sections, 22 songs, 6 full changes and 9 add-ons for Rihanna, 11 changes for 9 dancers, 5 changes for 2 singers and so on and so on... Oh, and duplicates of every outfit – around-the-clock work for weeks, and around 200 outfits that all need to be packed in 2 days. I've been working with Ri since the "Umbrella" days and I am impressed with, and proud of, the team. This show is going to be amazing and I can't wait to see it. Every day, the pieces of the puzzle come together, from choreography to the video montages on the LED screens on the stage, to props and lighting and of course the costumes. I look forward to the show getting on the road.'

Rihanna's third tour kicked off on 16 April 2010 and ran through to 12 March 2011. It was called 'The Last Girl on Earth Tour', and it was a world tour, with 73 dates. Rihanna named the tour 'The Last Girl on Earth' because that's the way she likes to think of herself. She explained to *Entertainment Tonight*: 'Sometimes people make decisions based on the outlook of others and you know, to me, my life is my life. It's my world and I'm going to live it the way I want to. That's how I think about everything; that way I'm focused on me and my work. It's a really narrow space, a focus.'

Rihanna had learned a lot from her 'Good Girl Gone Bad Tour', and was determined to make the new tour even better. She told AOL before the tour started: '[We've] never done a tour to this capacity. The production is unbelievable and the costumes, we just took it to a whole new level. Visually and sonically it's going to be a big step up from the last time. We just keep growing, and this time it is a massive production that I cannot wait for.'

The tour was put together by Jamie King and Simon Henwood, Rihanna's creative director. Her supporting acts this time around were Tinie Tempah, Tinchy Stryder, Pixie Lott, Travie, Ke$ha, DJ Daddy K, Vitaa, Vegas, DJ Ross Rosco, J Brazil, Alexis Jordan, Far East Movement and Calvin Harris.

Rihanna wore outfits by a number of designers, including the French designer Alexandre Vauthier. He designed the LED dress she wore at the start of the show, and she will often wear his creations to photo shoots and events. The long-sleeved nude minidress she wears in the video for 'Russian Roulette' and the black bodysuit she wears on the cover of her single 'Hard' are both Vauthier designs.

Rihanna loves staying up to date with the latest fashions, and she is the second biggest customer of the designer department store Barneys New York.

For most of the tour dates, her set list was:

1. 'Mad House' (via video)
2. 'Only Girl (In the World)'
3. 'Hard'
4. 'Shut Up and Drive'
5. 'Fire Bomb'
6. 'Disturbia'
7. 'Untitled I' (via video)
8. 'Rockstar 101'
9. 'S & M'
10. 'Rude Boy'
11. 'Hate That I Love You'
12. 'Love the Way You Lie Part II'
13. 'Unfaithful'
14. 'Te Amo'
15. 'What's My Name?'
16. 'Pon de Replay'
17. 'Untitled II' (via video)
18. 'Don't Stop the Music'
19. 'Breakin' Dishes'
20. 'Let Me'
21. 'S.O.S.'
22. 'Take A Bow'
23. Encore:
24. 'Untitled IV' (via video)
25. 'Wait Your Turn/ Live Your Life/ Run This Town' medley
26. 'Umbrella'

Some performers can be divas at times and make huge demands when they tour, but Rihanna isn't like that. Other stars want their dressing rooms redecorated, puppies to play with, snooker tables, full-length mirrors, new toilet seats and certain food and drinks laid on. Rihanna keeps things simple, and just has candles and incense in her dressing rooms.

Rihanna's tour guitarist is Nuno Bettencourt, a singer-songwriter who is best known for being the lead guitarist of the band Extreme. Normally, Rihanna's music doesn't contain a lot of guitar music, but for the tour she wanted to have more of a rock sound, which meant that she needed a talented guitarist. Nuno was the right man for the job, and because he wasn't busy with Extreme, he was able to commit wholeheartedly. He knew it would be challenging and different from anything he had done before, as he explained to journalist and metalhead Carl Begai: 'She wanted somebody to make things rock a little bit, which meant that I would basically get to do what I do if I took the job. I thought it was really interesting to be able to play my style of guitar over her stuff, I thought it would be fun, so I went for it. It's cool. I wouldn't have been interested if I wasn't able to be myself, and it's a challenge because the set is 24 or 25 songs that require a different sort of guitar playing to pull it off. At one point I'm playing pop stuff and making it a bit heavier, there's some funk and R&B, some ballads, some piano stuff, even some Hispanic flamenco, so it keeps things interesting. It certainly feels more at home than I thought it would.'

Nuno's favourite tracks to perform were 'Let Me' and 'S.O.S', although they sounded very different to the versions on her albums. He faced some criticism from fans of his own band, but he didn't mind – he just enjoyed spending time with Rihanna on the road, trying something different.

April was a great month for Rihanna, because she got to start her tour with Nuno and the rest of her band and dancers, and she loves performing every night for her fans. For the first two weeks of the tour, she had dates in Belgium, Holland, Switzerland, France and Germany. All her hard work paid off, because European fans loved the show.

Things nearly went horribly wrong when she injured herself after a performance in Switzerland. It was only her third performance of the tour. Her rib was hurting so badly that she was rushed to a private clinic so a doctor could take a look at it. Luckily, it wasn't broken or seriously damaged, so Rihanna was able to perform the next night in Lyon, France. She really is a trouper to keep performing, because lots of artists would have been tempted to cancel the concert and have a few days off to recuperate.

It was just as well things were okay, because after performing concerts in Europe, Rihanna had the North American leg of her tour to look forward to in the July.

Reading the reviews of the 'Last Girl on Earth Tour' from all around the world, clearly the critics were impressed by how much Rihanna had developed, and how the show continued the themes of the album. Mikael

Wood from *Rolling Stone* magazine was at the Los Angeles concert, which saw Eminem join Rihanna onstage. In his review, he wrote that Rihanna managed to hold 'the audience's attention throughout a nearly two-hour show full of costume changes, video bits and complicated set pieces like the one in "Te Amo", that had a pair of scantily-clad aerial dancers dangling from two giant machine guns. Military imagery cropped up regularly, from the pink tank Rihanna straddled while performing "Hard" to the gas-masked dancers flanking the singer during "S.O.S." Aggression was a general theme overall; near the end of "Shut Up and Drive", Rihanna pulled a young girl from the front row, gave her a bat and instructed her to beat the crap out of an old car that had appeared onstage. The singer also had Nuno Bettencourt of Extreme playing guitar, which gave much of the music a rowdy hard-rock vibe.'

The *Boston Globe*'s reviewer Sarah Rodman commented: 'Even amid the glittery circus that was her stage set, Rihanna, rocking a shock of fuchsia locks and a half-dozen form-fitting costumes, glided, strutted, and swanned through the eye of the storm with a natural grace and winking charm. Dancers spun around her on a jungle gym (Don't Stop the Music), aerialists dangled from big chrome guns (Te Amo), monsters on stilts encroached menacingly (Disturbia), and the singer even rocked a few guitar licks (Rockstar 101).'

Rihanna is such a good person to work with that lots of her dancers have been with her for years. Bryan Tanak started with her back in 2005, took part in the 'Umbrella' video, and is touring with her now, although he did have a break for a while. He is a dance teacher and has worked with Destiny's Child, Mariah Carey and Beyoncé.

Tanak was interviewed by Rihanna Daily, the official Rihanna fan site, and described what it is like to be Rihanna's dancer. He said: 'The best part about working for Rihanna is that she is the most caring, smart, and down-to-earth woman. Not to mention she's drop-dead gorgeous.

'The most interesting place we've played together was Abuja, Nigeria. The performance was kinda chaotic, due to lack of preparation from the Nigerian side. It got made up when Jay-Z took the stage with her, though. But the icing on it all was that half of our crew got stranded in Abuja for an extra 2 days and I missed our next show because of it!'

He also revealed: 'The funniest moment with Rihanna was on our last show of our first European tour. We played sooo many pranks onstage. The highlight was when me and Julius came out as Egyptian Pharaohs on "Question Existing". We made her crack up during her song!'

Several of Rihanna's dancers and choreographers are members of the talent agency Bloc. The people in charge posted this message on their official site when they were hired to work on the 'Last Girl on Earth Tour': 'Bloc choreographer Tanisha Scott with Luther Brown and Hollywood are currently in Los Angeles choreographing for Rihanna's upcoming tour. Congrats to bloc dancers Chase Benz, Khasan Brailsford and Whyley Yoshimura, who will join Rihanna on the road, starting with Europe in mid-April!'

Tanisha Scott is an amazing choreographer and dancer who hails from Canada, but has Jamaican roots. She first became famous as a choreographer when she worked on the video for Sean Paul's 'Gimme the Light' back in 2001, and since then she has choreographed lots of his videos as well as appearing in videos for Ne-Yo, Ludacris and Ciara. For her 'Last Girl on Earth Tour', Rihanna had eleven other choreographers and consultants in addition to Tanisha, and they were led by Jamie King.

Rihanna's dancers are the best of the best, and they have all proved they've got what it takes to support Rihanna. Individually, they have worked with P. Diddy, Britney Spears, Janet Jackson, Alicia Keys, Beyoncé and many more top artists. Rihanna's dancers have become part of her extended family, along with her stylists, drivers and people from her record company.

Bryan Tanak might have loved performing in Abuja, Nigeria, but Rihanna loved her Australian performances the best. She told the *Sunday Herald Sun*: 'Australia and New Zealand was my favourite, favourite leg of my last headline tour – it was awesome – so we're definitely coming back.

'Coming from Barbados, I think in terms of culture, we're very similar. But the tour is going to be massive in its overall look and feel, and the costumes are really cool.'

Rihanna might be one of the most attractive women in the world but she still has bad days. She has times when she feels really ugly and doesn't want to have her photo taken. As she revealed to *More!* magazine: 'I have an ugly day every month; pimples on my face, I'm fat and in a bad mood. It's more like an ugly week!'

Rihanna's fans would disagree, because they never see her looking bad, but they understand that every woman sometimes has insecurities. RiRi has never been fat, though, and most women would love to have her figure. She was slimmer when she released 'Pon de Replay' but that was because she was only 17, and as a girl becomes a woman, her body shape changes. When Rihanna was just starting out in the record business, she would put aside some time to do Pilates. She used to carry a workout DVD with her and worked out at least three times every week. Doing Pilates helped raise her endurance levels, her strength and her flexibility, too, which would have helped with her performances. Exercise also helps release tension, and makes everyone feel better about themselves.

RiRi confessed to *Us Magazine* back then that she usually had two meals a day. She would start her day with boiled egg whites, bacon and toast and have fish and rice for her lunch or dinner. She'd eat a granola bar, too. She told the magazine: 'I never acquired a taste for vegetables, because I didn't grow up eating them.' Rihanna eats more than two meals a day now because she has to. She burns so much energy that she would collapse if she didn't graze at times.

Touring keeps Rihanna fit, because she has to be able to perform for two hours without getting out of breath. She needs the stamina to be able to do this every night for weeks on end. Being friends with her dancers must help, too because she can follow their direction when it comes to the food she needs to eat to keep her body working properly. When she's touring, Rihanna has to keep her body in tip-top condition, which means she has to follow a diet of healthy eating. This is really hard for her, because she likes her food. She admitted to *More!* magazine: 'I've been working out a lot and I eat pretty boring – boiled egg, fruit, tons of water and some chicken. Well, this week I've eaten some other things but really small portions. I hate vegetables. I hate anything healthy, but if you want the results you've got to do it. I haven't even been drinking alcohol with dinner since I've been with this diet.'

Even when she's not touring, Rihanna is constantly running around from interview to interview, or to and from the recording studio. She has to eat on the move a lot, and sometimes just has to eat what she's given. Rihanna loves Spicy Nacho flavour Doritos (and spicy food in general), and makes sure she takes chilli with her when she goes out for food. She likes adding red pepper to meals to spice them up, and revealed in one interview that her make-up artist and friend Mylah Morales is fond of adding chilli, too.

RiRi's favourite restaurant has to be Giorgio Baldi in Los Angeles. It is open every day apart from Mondays, and she sometimes eats there five times in a week if she's at home. She loves their food so much that she would rather eat at 'Il Ristorante di Giorgio Baldi' than cook for herself or go to another restaurant. The paparazzi know how much she loves the place, and so they generally know where to find her when she's home; but they are not allowed to hassle her while she is eating: they just wait outside, ready for her to leave.

Rihanna loves Italian food very much, and her favourite meal has to be spaghetti. She has been trying to learn how to speak Italian for a while, but it isn't going very well – she's been too busy to study the Rosetta Stone language program that she got for a Christmas present. She knows how to swear in Italian, but that's about it!

Rihanna is constantly being told she is one of the sexiest women on the planet, but she still struggles to accept it. She told BBC Radio 1: 'I feel so flattered and never get used to it. Anytime I hear it, I feel it's a compliment. I had to learn to just go for it when it comes to being sexy, as I used to be self-conscious. Now I'm pretty solid and happy with my body, and what I'm uncomfortable with my body I accept it for what it is. At times I get bloated, a little bigger from time to time and a couple more dimples on the backs of my legs. You just have to learn to be happy with what you have.'

Playboy magazine has tried to convince her to strip off to grace its front cover a few times. So far she has turned them down, although she may do a nude photo shoot in the future, if and when she wants to. She would want to do this in a stylish and classy way, and would never do it for money.

In May 2009, Rihanna was devastated when nude photos she had taken for an ex-boyfriend ended up on the

Internet. It was only a short time after the photo of her beaten-up face had been leaked, and so it made RiRi feel even worse.

She confessed to the hosts of the New York City radio station Hot 97: 'It was the worst thing that could possibly ever happen to me. I just felt like my whole privacy was taken before that [the first leaked photo] and then, when that came out, I thought, "Oh great, so now there's nothing they don't know about me and my private life." It was humiliating and it was embarrassing – especially my mom having to see that.'

RiRi decided that she had to tell her mum before someone else did, and so she sent her some flowers before letting her know what had happened. The timing was terrible, as it was two days before Mother's Day. However, Monica loves RiRi no matter what, and once it was all out in the open, she helped her daughter cope.

Some women can be very cruel, and enjoy saying nasty things about Rihanna because they are jealous of the fact that men find RiRi so attractive. They say she dresses inappropriately, and is setting a bad example for young girls.

Rihanna knows what these people are saying, but doesn't let it bother her. She told *GQ*: 'People think I'm overly sexy. It bothers them for some reason. Girls don't like to see other girls dressed sexy. It's a little intimidating – I don't mean that in a cocky way.

'There's always going to be somebody not liking what you do. People have a lot of crazy opinions on things.

Things I say, things I wear, places I go. It's just stupid. It's bulls★★t. I'm a 22-year-old human being. It's fine for me to go to a club.

'People are hypocrites. They can't wait to say something horrible. Most of them are unhappy with themselves. It's women who are mad at other women. They should take a look at their own lives. A lot of people don't have the guts to confront themselves – they don't have the balls.'

Rihanna is going to continue to dress sexily, because it gives her confidence and makes her feel good. If she was wearing something unfeminine then it would have a negative impact on her performance, and fans would notice immediately. Fashion is one of her passions, so she is always going to want to wear the latest items from the catwalk. RiRi knows that her beauty won't last forever, so she's appreciating how her body looks now. However, she can see both sides of the argument and admitted: 'Public figures can become annoying. They see me a lot, and every time they see me, my ass is out or my boobs are out so it can get a little irritating, I get that. But I have to do what makes me happy, what I feel like doing.'

May 2010 saw Matt Kemp admit that he was dating Rihanna. She had been to watch him play for the Los Angeles Dodgers a few times and to support him, which was only fair because he had done the same for her. A few weeks earlier, she had spoken publicly about their relationship, and now it was his turn.

Matt was at a charity bowling event in Los Angeles when he was interviewed by *Us* magazine. He told them:

'Yeah! That's my girl! She's just a fun person. I love to be around her.'

Rihanna was not at the event because she was busy touring, so Matt was looking forward to seeing her when she next had some time off. He said: 'She's definitely not gonna be here for a little while. She's definitely a great person in my life, and I'm happy I'm with her.'

At the end of May, Rihanna released 'Rockstar 101', the fourth single from *Rated R*. The track includes a guitar solo by Guns N' Roses guitarist Slash and was written by The-Dream and Tricky Stewart. It came out on 25 May.

The video was directed by Melina Matsoukas, and Travis Barker from Blink-182 played the drummer in Rihanna's rock band. He actually taught Rihanna how to play and told MTV: 'She's awesome! I haven't seen anyone catch on that quick in quite a while and have that kind of ear for drums or rhythm, so I was stoked that she could really play the drums.' As well as wearing some very sexy outfits in the video, Rihanna put on a Slash-style outfit and played around with a guitar before smashing it to pieces. In one scene she wears a crown and is covered in black body paint, with chains wrapped around her, and in another, she wanders through a forest in the snow.

When people heard 'Rockstar 101' for the first time, they were impressed that the former Guns N' Roses guitarist had collaborated with Rihanna on the track. She had approached Slash after a Black Eyed Peas charity concert to ask if he was interested in working with her. Rihanna was so busy that they didn't meet in a studio to work on the track together, and instead recorded their sections separately.

She had originally planned that Slash himself would be in the video, but he pulled out because he had been putting in the hours preparing for his own track to come out, and he believed that 'Rockstar 101' would be a hit with or without him in the video. He felt that the finished video was great, and told Rihanna he rated it in a text. As he revealed to MTV: 'All things considered, it brings an element of sexuality to it that I probably wouldn't have been capable of. I think it's hot, and I sent her a text this morning telling her it was definitely hotter with her doing it than with me doing it. Everything works out the way it's supposed to.

'I'm way more flattered that she played me in the video than her asking me to be in it,' he said. 'All things considered, she's pretty cool.'

An album containing 12 remixes of the song was released on May 25, each having been remixed by a different artist.

In June 2010, Rihanna released 'Te Amo' from the *Rated R* album for her international fans. Written by Rihanna, Stargate and James Fauntleroy II, when translated from the Spanish/Portuguese the title means 'I love you'. It is a song about desire, and Rihanna is being pursued by a female admirer. It was No. 1 in Bulgaria and charted in the UK at No. 14, No. 9 in Switzerland, No. 11 in German and No. 14 in Finland.

Digital Spy gave the track four out of five stars, saying in its review: 'One of her *Rated R* LP's less menacing moments, "Te Amo" finds La Fenty grappling with her sexuality over some irresistible, Latin-infused Stargate beats. However, after realising *precisely* what her same sex suitor means when she says "te amo", she has no choice but to let her down gently: "I feel love but I don't feel that way." Oh Ri, you're officially the world's biggest heartbreaker.'

Rihanna filmed the video in late April in the Château de Vigny in France. The actress who played her lover was a French model called Laetitia Casta, and it was directed by Anthony Mandler. While she was in France to film the video, Rihanna told the *Daily Mirror* how much she was missing Matt. She said: 'I'm really happy right now. Paris is an amazing city. I love it. It would have been so cool if he was here.

'I was hoping he would be able to come to London but he's working. And I'm touring and shooting videos for my next single so it's going to be seven weeks before I see him again.

'It'll probably be when I get back to America that we can hook up properly. We have to make do with Skype and phone, but I miss him. And this is the most romantic town. I can't wait to see him again.'

She also spoke to *Elle* magazine about how much Matt had changed her life and helped her through her troubles. She told them: 'I have a boyfriend. I'm so happy. I feel really comfortable, and it's so easy. I have such a chaotic life, but at the end of the day, that is just my peace. It keeps me sane, really, talking to him and talking to my family.'

Rihanna is a person who loves music, and when she's travelling she will listen to her favourite tracks. Some of the tracks she loves are written and sung by some of her closest friends, so she finds extra meaning behind them. RiRi believes that music is in her DNA. She does have some of her own records in her playlist, but she also enjoys tracks by Miley Cyrus, John Mayer and Kings of Leon. Rihanna first heard Amy Winehouse's music when she was in London and she was impressed by it. She was also surprised that it took another year for it to be played in the US. In the past, she has admitted that she likes the wide variety of music that is played in the UK, because she finds it much more diverse than in the US.

When she was interviewed by iTunes, she revealed what her playlist at the time looked like:

'Best I Ever Had' by Drake
'Closer' by Kings of Leon
'Young Forever' by Jay-Z featuring Mr Hudson
'Venus vs. Mars' by Jay-Z
'Meet Me Halfway' by Black Eyed Peas
'La La La' by LMFAO
'Throw it in the Bag' (Remix) by Fabolous featuring Drake and The-Dream
'Party in the U.S.A' by Miley Cyrus
'Thinking of You' by Katy Perry
'Umbrella' by Rihanna featuring Jay-Z
'Russian Roulette' by Rihanna
'Sweet Dreams' by Beyoncé
'Waiting on the World to Change' by John Mayer

Other artists that Rihanna likes include Bob Marley, Paramore and Trey Songz.

She also talked about the first time she went to a big concert. Back in 2004, she went to the Ladies First Tour, and was thrilled to have the opportunity to see Beyoncé, Missy Elliot and Alicia Keys on the same night (the three singers had joined together because they hadn't wanted to do solo tours on their own). Beyoncé had been used to performing with the other members of Destiny's Child, so she liked having the support of Missy Elliot and Alicia Keys.

Rihanna told iTunes: 'I was in like, a nosebleed seat but I was in tears. I could not believe that Beyoncé was right there, and Alicia Keys and Missy Elliott.

'I was a little starstruck. No, I was very starstruck, but it was so much fun. It was very inspiring and it motivated me so much.'

These performers now consider RiRi their equal, and in Beyoncé's case, the two are now friends. It is crazy how things can change in just a few years.

If RiRi had to choose one song as the soundtrack to her life she says it would have to be a medley of Bob Marley's 'Waiting In Vain', 'Girls Just Wanna Have Fun' by Cyndi Lauper, and 'F★★★ You' by Cee-Lo Green.

One of her big musical ambitions is to play at the Glastonbury music festival. She has wanted to perform there ever since Jay-Z headlined, back in June 2008. He helped introduce more R&B to the Glastonbury mix, and RiRi would love to follow in his footsteps.

She confided in Q Magazine: 'I'd love to play

Glastonbury. I have heard so many things about what happens there. I love rock music. I love Kings of Leon and The Prodigy. You could have nightmares about that guy with the clown face and the weird hair [Keith Flint]. That's a look to scare little kids, right?

'But the music is awesome. I like the more traditional rock bands, too: Aerosmith and Bon Jovi. I think I could rock the stage at Glastonbury, no question.'

HEAR
MY CRY

Rihanna collaborated with Eminem on his track 'Love the Way You Lie', which was the second single from his album, *Recovery*. It was released on 8 June 2010 and quickly became the most successful collaboration Rihanna had ever done: it was No. 1 in 16 countries and was at the top of the US charts for seven consecutive weeks.

In the UK, 'Love the Way You Lie' only reached No. 2 in the charts, but ended up becoming the bestselling single of 2010. It was also the second bestselling single of 2010 in Canada. To date, it has sold more than nine million copies worldwide.

Rihanna and Eminem performed the track together at the 2010 MTV Video Music Awards and during the 21 July performance of Rihanna's 'Last Girl on Earth Tour'. They also performed it at the 2011 Grammy Awards: they had been nominated for five awards that night but didn't win any of them. However, they did pick up the Best Rap/Hip-Hop Track Award at the Teen Choice Awards, Best Song Hip-Hop of the Year at the Soul Train Awards, and Favourite Music Video and Favourite Song at the People's Choice Awards.

In the video Rihanna and Eminem appear in some scenes, but the main story scenes were done by Megan Fox and Dominic Monaghan. Fox and Monaghan play lovers in an abusive relationship, who become physical, fight, steal and drink too much. It is clear that they should separate, but they don't, because they love each other. In Rihanna's scenes she sings outside the couple's burning house, and the video ends with Eminem, Fox and Monaghan engulfed by flames. It was the first video Rihanna filmed with bright red hair.

The video became a record breaker when it was released on YouTube, as it had 6.6 million views in the first 24 hours, the most any video has ever had. Fans of both Rihanna and Eminem loved the track, and the wider music world also rated the video. It was considered so good that it could have been the trailer for a big blockbuster movie.

The track was so popular that they recorded 'Love the Way You Lie (Part II)', which had Rihanna singing the majority of the lyrics, with Eminem taking the supporting role. Rihanna hadn't wanted to do this in the beginning because she felt that the first version had been so perfect that the Part II version would just look second best. Eventually Eminem was able to convince her to do

SARAH OLIVER

so and the track they produced ended up being just as good as the first. They produced a few more versions in the end, one with just a piano accompaniment and another with just drums. Eventually, Rihanna liked 'Love the Way You Lie (Part II)' so much that she included it in her next album, *Loud*.

RiRi might have collaborated with Eminem, but he hasn't become her best friend or anything, and their relationship is purely business-based. When *Q Magazine* asked her to tell them something they didn't know about him, she couldn't think of anything and replied: 'Believe me, he is a mystery even to those who spend time with him. He is very reserved and he keeps things to himself. When he sent "Love The Way You Lie" to me, I thought it was an amazing song. Truly amazing lyrically, and that is what he is known for. That's the reason why I did it. I have become numb to the idea that I am going to get sh*t for doing things that push boundaries and go to the edge. The song does go to the edge because he has a past and I have experienced bad things in the past.

'It was a great piece of music and I went with it. Eminem is cool. Could I ring him for a chat? No, unless it's about music. He doesn't do a lot of small talk.'

GOING
RED

Rihanna's hairstylist is called Ursula Stephen; she is one of the best celebrity stylists in the world. She has coloured and cut the hair of Keyshia Cole and Michelle Williams (of Destiny's Child fame), but Rihanna is the client she is best known for styling.

Back in September 2008, Ursula told *People* magazine: 'Her hair is so versatile. Spiked up, all forward, slick it back, she rocks!' Fans all around the world had started to ask their hairdressers to give them 'the Rihanna', which amazed Ursula and RiRi because they never expected her short hairstyle to become iconic.

Rihanna has vowed never again to have her hair long and light brown as it was for 'Pon de Replay', because it didn't reflect who she wanted to be: she feels it was too generic. She has to get approval from her people before she makes any huge changes to her appearance, though, so they had to give her the thumbs-up first before she dyed her hair red. In one interview, she admitted that colouring her hair pink, purple or green was out of the question. When she first rebelled and cut her hair, they just made her wear hair extensions instead, which defeated the whole point of RiRi cutting her hair in the first place.

Since then, Rihanna has experimented with lots of different hairstyles, but when she made the decision to go red in June 2010, the whole world started talking about it. Ursula added real hair extensions dyed red to Rihanna's own hair, and used Motions Silkening Shine Relaxer System to keep it looking in tip-top condition.

Having long hair again, after having it short for so long, was quite irritating for Rihanna when she wanted to get some sleep. It keeps getting in the way, and so she uses a scarf to control it while she sleeps.

Rihanna finds red hair liberating, and enjoys the attention she gets from having such bright hair. She told SugarScape: 'With my hair I was ready for something new, something loud, something expressive and something fun. I'd had blonde hair and it was so boring for me.

'Black is still my favourite colour, but this time I wanted something edgier because I don't like the edgy clothes anymore. I guess I had to take the edge to somewhere else – my hair!'

For Rihanna's hairstylist Ursula Stephen, filming music videos can sometimes be a nightmare; however, she enjoyed the creative freedom she was given for her client's hair in the 'S & M' video, which was filmed in the middle of January 2010. She admitted to StyleList: 'Rihanna had all kinds of crazy ideas for that video and I went all out, buying like six different wigs, colouring them, cutting them. Music videos are usually my least favourite to do because there is so much pressure and such a rush, and then they wear the look for like, two minutes. But this was a creative challenge for me, so I loved it.'

Fans are sometimes shocked that RiRi wears a lot of wigs, but most celebrities do so because it protects their real hair from getting damaged. RiRi is constantly changing her hairstyles (from one day to the next sometimes), so Ursula can use wigs to give her the exact look she wants without having to touch her own hair, which is hidden underneath. The wigs Ursula gives RiRi to wear can vary enormously in price; some are only $20 but others cost thousands. She cuts and styles them in the same way that you would do with natural hair.

Even when Rihanna's not working, she likes to wear wigs, and after they finished the 'S & M' video she was careful to pack the fizzy afro curls wig, and took it on holiday with her. She likes her hair to complement her outfits and to make a statement.

Ursula explains to journalist Grace Gold how the style RiRi wants dictates what type of wig is chosen: 'It's not about the cost, or even if it's synthetic or real hair: it's about the style you want first. You have to have your vision then you go and find the piece. The only thing I'd say is a better choice is to go with synthetic hair if you want a real curly style. It holds much better.

'People say to me, "Why did you make her hair so big? Why is it so crazy out there?" But you have to understand: She's a performer. She can't just walk around with some little ponytail. She has to perform. She has to have an image. The hair even helps her get into the character of whatever she's doing.'

In order for RiRi to look great, it is important that everyone on her style team, her hair stylist, her make-up artist and her clothing stylist all work together to get her look just right: she needs her hair to complement her outfit, which needs to complement her make-up, and so on. She also needs to feel happy with her look so that she can go out and perform, whether that is on stage or on a red carpet. And before Rihanna steps onto the red carpet, she uses Motions Hold & Shine Styling Spray to make sure her hair looks perfect.

As well as being close to Ursula, Rihanna is also close to her make-up team because of the amount of time they spend together. Even when they're not working, they will go out for a bite to eat together or just hang out.

One of her make-up artists is Karin Darnell, who has worked with Victoria Beckham, the Sugababes, Peter Andre, Katie Price, Anastacia and George Michael in the past. She started doing Rihanna's make-up when she was in the UK and in Europe five years ago, and since then she's joined the main style team and does Rihanna's make-up wherever she travels around the world.

Because Karin has worked with Rihanna for so long, she has seen her develop musically and as a woman. She talked to RihannaDaily about meeting Rihanna all those years ago: 'I was certain Rihanna would turn out to be a major artist, but as an English make-up artist based in London, I could never have anticipated my future role in her image! And I feel truly blessed and genuinely enjoy the creative process working alongside Ursula (hair) and Mariel and Rob (stylists) and of course with Rihanna herself!'

Rihanna understands how powerful make-up can be in creating a look, and isn't afraid to push the boundaries and experiment. When her hair changed to red, her make-up had to change, too, as Karin explains: 'Along with the amazing red hair, a make-up change is always sure to follow! Every hairstyle, outfit change and event dictates a make-up moment!!! Always less obvious than the hair, but always there, nevertheless! Ursula and I love to work together, we "push" each other hard! It's great! The "new look" is softer than ever before! There are no hard lines or dark eyes! Just soft pastel, feminine eyes with fluttery lashes! Colours don't need to match, maybe just surprise you a little with an unusual colour wash or hue! Sometimes I like to bring out the red lip for impact! And that's enough!'

If you want to learn how to do your make-up like Rihanna, you need to head over to YouTube and check out the amazing tutorials that fans have done, which show you, step-by-step, how to recreate Rihanna's look in the different music videos. If her own make-up artist is impressed by how accurate they are, then you should be pleased with the results if you follow their advice.

Several of Rihanna's videos have been directed by Anthony Mandler, the man behind Nelly Furtado's 'Maneater', Fergie's 'Big Girls Don't Cry' and John Mayer's 'Heartbreak Warfare'. He has also directed videos for Jay-Z, Ciara, Mariah Carey, Snoop Dogg, Beyoncé and many more big stars.

Mandler was first brought on board to direct 'Unfaithful' in 2006, but he has done several more of RiRi's videos since then. He directed 'We Ride', 'Shut Up and Drive', 'Hate That I Love You', 'Take A Bow', 'Disturbia', 'Rehab', 'Russian Roulette', 'Wait Your Town', 'Te Amo', 'Only Girl (In the World)' and 'California King Bed'.

He has also directed Rihanna in videos when she has collaborated with other artists. In 2008, he directed the Maroon 5 video for 'If I Never See Your Face Again' and T.I.'s video for 'Live Your Life'. Then, in 2009, he directed Jay-Z's 'Run This Town' video, which also stars Kanye West.

Def Jam liked some of the videos that Mandler had directed previously and wanted him to reinvent Rihanna. Once Mandler met her, they formed a friendship that has got stronger and stronger as time passed. Anthony talked to Rap-Up.com about what it was like in the beginning. He said: 'We just really connected. From that point on, it was "Unfaithful". She saw me as someone who could support and drive her artistry and personality, eventually in a more sexual and womanly way. I saw it as an opportunity to work with somebody in the capacity of a muse – I really look at her like that. I feel like we've grown through each other, around each other, and because of each other, and will never take back the quality of work or the freedom that she's given me to communicate. You kill for stuff like that in an artist, especially in this medium, which is filled with disloyalty and criticism. I can't tell you how many No. 1 videos I've had where the artist went somewhere else after: she's the ultimate in loyalty.'

To date, his two favourite Rihanna videos are 'Disturbia' and 'Russian Roulette'. He explained why: '"Disturbia" was the one that everybody said would ruin her career from the inside out. People were not supportive of that video and it took myself, Rihanna and my partner Ciarra Pardo to defend it and push it forward – move the needle as far as what was okay and not okay with a girl like her. It really broadened and opened her brand. "Russian Roulette" because it's obviously a piece of the pie of what happened and it was the way to tell an intense story that obviously had a lot behind it. She really gave me free rein. I had a dream about her being underwater and these people shooting at her and bullets whipping by her and grazing her. I woke up and called her and said, "I got this idea. You gotta tell me what the song is." At that point, I don't even think the song had been made yet. To be able to have a moment like that, and be able to call one of the biggest stars in the world and pitch that to them, and then have them saying, "Let's do it", it's such a blessing. Every artist dreams of having that kind of outlet.'

Rihanna might really admire Anthony's work, but she also

uses other directors. Melina Matsoukas directed 'Rude Boy', 'Hard', 'Rockstar 101' and 'S & M' (alongside Rihanna).

It seems that everyone who has worked with Rihanna regards her as a great singer and a nice person, too. Makeba Riddick is one of Rihanna's core people, and also one of the best producers and songwriters in the world.

Makeba started out working for Jennifer Lopez and the band B2K back in 2002, but since then, she has worked with a whole host of big stars: Mariah Carey, Toni Braxton, Beyoncé, Kelis and the Sugababes, to name but a few. The first song she worked on with Rihanna was the T.I. Track, 'Live Your Life'. Since then she has helped produce and write songs for four of Rihanna's albums.

She revealed to *Us* magazine: 'I was there from the beginning, from the week she got signed before she even had a record deal. I was one of the first people she went into the studio with. It is always a wild adventure with her. Rihanna travels a lot, and she loves to have her people with her. We listen to music, we watch videos, we drink champagne – it's literally a party in the studio with her all of the time and it's fun.

'She's very witty and definitely an easy person to work with. Although she's an international superstar, we've had a relationship for so many years now that it's like going in the studio with a cousin. It doesn't feel like work at all.'

If Makeba had to pick a favourite song out of all the ones she has written or produced, she would have to choose 'Live Your Life' because of the fun she had in Italy recording it with T.I. and Rihanna, and because it did so well in the charts. It managed to stay at the top of the charts for 10 weeks, which is a personal record for Makeba.

During the interview with *Us* magazine she talked about two special times she has shared with Rihanna. She admitted: 'We were in Hawaii last year and we were on these paddle-boards. Everyone we were with was falling into the water and it was hilarious, but Rihanna was the only one that was able to keep her balance. We're all soaking wet, drenched with water, hair all over the place and that really stood out to me because it was so much fun. Another time we were in London, working on the *Rated R* album, and there was a sushi spot we love that they shut down for us. Jay-Z and all his Rock Nation people were there and we turned that place into a club. It always just feels like family with her and her people.'

HELPING
SHANNON

In July 2010, Rihanna found out about a young actress called Shannon Tavarez, who had been diagnosed with an aggressive form of leukaemia three months earlier, aged eleven. Shannon had been playing Nala in the Broadway production of *The Lion King* when she started getting pains in her legs. After visiting the doctor, she was diagnosed with leukaemia and the race was on to find her a bone marrow match, because she desperately needed a transplant. Because her dad was Dominican and her mom was African-American, this wasn't going to be easy.

Rihanna wanted to do something for her, and along with Alicia Keys and 50 Cent, she appealed to her fans for help. She told *People* magazine: '[Shannon] should be performing on Broadway, but is confined to her bed, fighting for her life.

'She needs to find a bone marrow donor to survive. I urge all my fans to register (as donors). It's the most beautiful thing someone could do, to give the gift of life.'

Sadly a bone marrow match couldn't be found for Shannon, and she had an umbilical cord blood transplant in August 2010. She died from leukaemia on 1 November 2010, and the lights at the theatre where *The Lion King* was being staged were dimmed. Her mum released a statement, which read: 'Shannon's dream was to perform on stage, and that she did.'

When Rihanna heard the news that Shannon had died, she was understandably upset. She tweeted: 'Just got off of a plane ride and got horrible news that our little star Shannon Tavarez has lost her battle against leukaemia. Way too soon. Keep her family in your prayers.'

TOURING IN THE US — WITH KE$HA

Rihanna hit the road again for the North America and Canada part of her tour, which took place in 26 cities over July and August 2010. She was joined by her support act Ke$ha, and they had fun together, as Ke$ha divulged to MTV: 'We have slumber parties and pillow fights, and we braid each other's hair a lot.

'We talk about boys, naked. Touring with Rihanna is incredible, you should come see it. It's really fun. I've been out with her for about two weeks now and I just learn so much from her as a performer. She has one of the best voices of anyone I've ever seen live and I kind of just take it as my opportunity to hype up thousands of people. It's epic. She's amazing live and her voice is just so good. I'm kind of just, like, her hype girl. I take the stage and hype it up for 40 minutes.'

FACT FILE – KE$HA

Ke$ha is a singer-songwriter most famous for her tracks 'Tik Tok' and 'We R Who We R'. Before getting her own record deal, she sang backing vocals for Britney Spears and Paris Hilton, and appeared in a Katy Perry video. Her big break came when she provided the female voice on the Flo Rida track, 'Right Round'.

Since January 2010, she has sold more than two million albums, and getting the opportunity to be one of Rihanna's supporting acts was a great way for her to show the world what she could do. Three months after she finished her 'Last Girl On Earth' dates, she announced her first tour.

One night of the tour that stands out for Rihanna, her dancers and crew is 25 August. That was the night her dancer Chase Benz decided to propose to his girlfriend. Tessa Reyes had gone to see the concert in Chicago without knowing that her boyfriend would be making her go on stage. Everyone behind the scenes was in on it and they posted up three photos on the background screen before Chase got down on one knee. One photo had Chase as a little kid, another had the young Tessa and the third photo was a recent picture of the two together. After Tessa said 'yes', the audience cheered and the couple walked off together backstage, where no doubt RiRi congratulated them.

The people close to Rihanna enjoyed other special nights, too. Kanye West saw her performance at New York's Madison Square Garden and was amazed. That night, he himself was performing at a secret show at the Bowery Ballroom, but he couldn't resist popping in to see Rihanna's show first. He felt he had to share how good Rihanna's concert was with his audience, and told them: 'So I went to Rihanna's concert tonight and when I saw her do "I'm so hard, eh eh eh", I'm not gonna lie to ya'll, I might have actually started crying, just to see my little sister onstage with her production, her outfit, her song and rocking Madison Square Garden at her own sold-out show. It was a very emotional moment for me and I'm just so proud of her.'

Rihanna was on top form as she performed to sell-out crowds each night, and then Billboard announced that with 'Love the Way You Lie' at No. 1, she was tying with Beyoncé, Mariah Carey and Lady Gaga for the artist with the most No. 1 singles on the pop airplay chart.

Despite being really busy with her tour, Rihanna continued to go and see Matt play for his baseball team whenever she could. From June onwards his performances hadn't been as good as usual, and he began being placed on the bench. Los Angeles Dodgers fans started to blame Rihanna and said his poor form was down to him spending too much time with her. They thought Matt's girlfriend being in the stands might also affect him on match days.

Matt heard the rumours and decided to set the record straight. He told the *Los Angeles Times*: 'My girl has nothing to do with what I do on the baseball field. If anything, she helps. She makes me happy, and as stressed as I am coming home sometimes, it's nice to have someone there who just wants to support you.'

Because Rihanna only has time to visit Barbados a couple of times a year, she enjoys getting to know other Bajans who cross her path. She spent some time in the recording studio with Shontelle in the summer of 2010, having previously worked with her back in 2007 on the J-Status track, 'Roll It'. They had originally met when they were both kids growing up in Barbados. Shontelle was actually Rihanna's drill sergeant for a time, and explains on her official website: 'There was one occasion when I had to make her drop and give me ten push-ups. We laugh about it now, I think she's forgiven me.'

Shontelle was also signed by Evan Rogers and Carl Sturken, after they heard one of her tracks being played by a Bajan radio station, and soon afterwards, she ended up moving to the US. Because she comes from the same country, and she was signed by the two men who signed Rihanna, many people have suggested that the two performers are enemies but this couldn't be farther from the truth.

During a promotional trip to the UK in August 2010 before her single 'Impossible' came out, Shontelle explained to Digital Spy: 'People want to make us enemies so bad and we just laugh about it because we're like, I don't get it. We are two girls from Barbados who are just so excited about the fact that we come from this small island that so many people didn't even know existed until Rihanna broke out.

'Now we recently made history, where we had two artists from Barbados in the Top 10 at the same time – and that has never happened ever in history, not even from any country outside the US. So we're so excited that our little island is making such great waves, you know. I mean, we just love it and we've recently been in the studio together and we just keep laughing like, wow, we're rivals but yet we're working together.'

Shontelle actually helped Rihanna pen the track 'Man Down' for her *Loud* album, alongside Timothy and Theron Thomas and Shama Joseph. In order to squeeze in the time to do this because of Rihanna's hectic schedule, Shontelle went to watch one of her concerts, and the second it was over, Rihanna came and sat in one of the buses and they started to write it. Because Shontelle knew RiRi so well, she found writing the song a lot easier than it would have been writing for someone she didn't know.

Rihanna loved the finished song because it had such a Jamaican vibe.

TWITTER

Up until August 2010, Rihanna's Twitter account was controlled by her record label: she decided things had to change and so she took over. Once the switch had been made, she tweeted: 'So now that i finally took over my Twitter page no more corny label tweets......lol! whaaasssuupppp ppl!!!!!'

Rihanna told BBC Radio 1: 'I'm still not a big Twitter person but I tweet now and then when I have to or when I want to say what's up to my fans. I like talking to my fans, but then I don't want to be overdoing it and tweeting all the time. I hate it when people tweet all the time, every second, it annoys me and I wouldn't like to be that annoying person. I don't think anyone is that interested, anyway.'

She wanted to start interacting with her fans properly for

the first time and ask for their advice on things she should and shouldn't do. When she first started tweeting, RiRi worried a lot about what she should write, and thought about what she would tweet for days, but now she is fine about it and just tweets what she thinks.

Rihanna's fans love the fact that she can be a bit crazy at times and isn't afraid to make mistakes. She isn't scared to tweet things that might annoy her record company, either: she is a rebel at times and wants her fans to express themselves and be happy all the time. RiRi genuinely cares for them and wants them to be comfortable in their own skin. She often uses Twitter to tell them to be true to themselves.

Around the same time as taking control of her own Twitter account, Rihanna started looking on fan forums and joined a live chat on her official fansite RihannaDaily.com. As she joined in the debate, fans accused her of being an imposter; she made one of her friends contact the site to verify it really was her.

Rihanna has always wanted to act in a movie but she's never been interested in playing a singer. When she found out about a new sci-fi movie based on the board game Battleship, she was interested because the story sounded fascinating, and she wasn't about to secure a super-glam role. She would need to act!

The movie was to be directed by Peter Berg, who is best known for directing *Hancock*, *The Rundown* and *The Kingdom*. *Batman Begins* actor Liam Neeson, Taylor Kitsch (*X-Men Origins: Wolverine*) and actor Alexander Skarsgård

(*Generation Kill*) were signed up, so it was to be a huge movie. It was a big challenge for Rihanna to take on, but she had wanted to be an actress for so long that she was willing to do whatever was needed.

Rihanna started filming her scenes in Hawaii in September 2010. She was to play Raikes, a weapons officer in the United States Navy. Her role is that of a tough girl who joins in the battleship fight against an alien enemy. Rihanna decided to tone down her Bajan accent for the movie: in interviews, she sometimes gets tired of being asked to answer the same questions three times because the interviewer can't understand what she is saying, so she didn't want to take any risks. She didn't want people saying they couldn't understand her after watching the movie in cinemas.

Entertainment Weekly asked Rihanna who was the most bad-ass in the movie out of herself, Alexander Skarsgård or Liam Neeson. She replied: 'Me. Well, the most bad-ass in the whole movie is Taylor Kitsch but I get to kick some ass, too.'

Initially, she had only two weeks of filming to do, and she flew in her friends and family so that they could have a bit of a holiday together before she had to go back to work. While she was there, she tweeted a photo of herself wearing leis (Hawaiian flower necklaces). During the holiday, everyone messed around with tattoo transfers and Rihanna had a huge gun transfer on her thigh. They hit the beach, and she ended up having fun in a canoe with Melissa. After returning home she had a busy few weeks, as she was promoting 'Only Girl (In the World)' and organising Katy Perry's bachelorette party. RiRi and Katy had grown particularly close over the previous year, and they had become the best of friends, not forgetting Melissa, of course.

Having been a cadet when she was growing up helped RiRi when it came to playing Raikes in *Battleship,* as she was able to impress both cast and crew with her weaponry skills. She talked to Q *Magazine* about what it was like to be part of the Bajan army cadet force: 'I was very good at drill – I had to be. The people I looked up to were really fit. I wanted to gain their respect. Sonita, my best friend at the time, did it with me. We got separated for talking and then we got good. I wasn't considering a career. It was a choice between Guides, Scouts and Cadets.

'I could probably drop and give you 20 easily but I'm not going to do it right now because I am wearing a tight dress, and it's late and I'm tired. I am pretty good with a rifle, too, and it has come in useful. I'm making a movie at the moment [*Battleship*] and I showed them I could already handle a weapon. They were blown away. Not literally, I've never fired a weapon in anger.'

In order to become an actress and not look like a singer trying to act, RiRi got herself an acting coach to work with her and teach her how to use what she has been through in the past to help portray emotions onscreen. She also learned more through watching other actresses in movies. Rihanna's favourite actresses are

Naomi Watts, Nicole Kidman and Meryl Streep. Her favourite male actors of the moment are Jonah Hill and Michael Cera.

The director Pete Berg must have been impressed by how much dedication Rihanna showed; it would have been easy for her not to put as much effort in, because she was so busy promoting her albums and singles between filming her scenes.

Rihanna really respects him, too, and told *Q Magazine* what she thought when she first signed up: 'Peter Berg is a genius. A movie based on a board game? How is that going to work? But I loved the script and it was perfect for my first role. I am a bad-ass tatted-up character called Weapons Officer Raikes. I know all there is to know about weapons on that ship. Can I act? Of course, but I am not telling you where I draw the experiences from. What do I think of when I want to do "angry"? That would be telling my secrets.'

Originally Berg had wanted to have Rihanna wear a navy cap in some scenes and then take it off for others but she looked too gorgeous without her cap and so he changed his mind. She kept it on and her hairstylist hardly had to do a thing.

Rihanna might have a body to die for but she herself has only started liking it in the last year or two. She has learned to embrace her womanly shape, and confessed to *Vogue* that the change came when she was preparing to play Raikes. She told them: 'For the first time, I don't want to get rid of the curves. I just want to tone it up. My body is comfortable, and it's not unhealthy, so I'm going to rock with it.

'Over the holidays, and even during filming, I realised that I actually like my body, even if it's not perfect according to the book. I just feel sexy.'

Rihanna's co-actors rated her performance highly too, with Josh Pence telling MTV: 'I had a scene with Rihanna. She was great! She brought it.

'She came in, and I respect the fact that she's willing to put a lot on the line, and it's like Justin [Timberlake] with *The Social Network*. You know, they've got a lot to lose and a lot of people judging them. It takes a lot of courage.'

Josh plays Chief Moore, a combat systems co-ordinator, in *Battleship*. RiRi, Josh and the rest of the cast couldn't wait for the movie to hit cinemas, so they must have been disappointed when the release date was pushed back to May 2012 instead of coming out in 2011 as originally planned.

On 19 December 2010, Rihanna tweeted: 'I'm officially wrapped from Battleship! I'm gonna miss it, but it's good to be home!'

She had finished her final filming stint in the last few weeks of November at Baton Rouge, Louisiana, but she knew she would be on a film set again. She was looking forward to seeing what other scripts and parts she was offered, because she gets such a buzz from acting. She wants to be known as a great singer and actress!

KATY PERRY

Melissa Forde might be Rihanna's best friend in the whole world, but Katy Perry must come a close second. Katy first burst onto the music scene in early 2008, and pretty soon afterwards she became friends with Rihanna. They would be at the same awards shows and events, and after meeting up a few times they realised they were going to become really good friends.

In April 2009 Rihanna invited Katy to go back home with her to Barbados and they had a girls' holiday. They went out in a boat and hung around with RiRi's friends from home. When they were in the US, Katy would invite RiRi around to her place and RiRi would do the same.

Katy and Rihanna are great friends and don't feel under pressure to be better than one another. They recognise that they both offer different things to their fans, as Katy explained to *Harper's Bazaar*: 'We're all unique. That's why we all win and we all can exist. People don't want just vanilla, they want 31 flavours. I couldn't do what Rihanna does. I couldn't do what Gaga does. They can't do what I do.'

During one interview RiRi was supposed to have said: 'I didn't want the generic pop record that Ke\$ha or Lady Gaga or Katy Perry would do – every song was tailored to me.' Some people took this as Rihanna saying Katy just produces 'generic pop'. However, RiRi was upset that people got the wrong impression from the quote and insisted it was taken out of context.

She told *Fabulous* magazine: 'I didn't say that – did you see the interview? That's not what I said. Okay, if anything it was a diss to songwriters and producers who can't make anything other than formula records. They'll make a song and give it to Rihanna. If she doesn't take it, they'll give it to Katy, and if Katy doesn't take it, they'll give it to Gaga. That's not what we want. We like songs that scream our individuality. We like records that speak for who we are as artists and that are tailored to us.'

FACT FILE – KATY PERRY

Katy Perry is a singer from Santa Barbara in California. Like Rihanna, she uses a stage name; her real name is Katheryn Elizabeth Hudson. She started her career using the name Katy Hudson, and made a gospel album and a solo album that were never released, before changing her stage name to Katy Perry and signing with Capitol Music Group in 2007. This was actually her fourth record label and, compared with Rihanna, she had a much rockier road to the top.

Her single 'I Kissed a Girl' was a massive hit in 2008 and from then on, she hasn't looked back. She has released two albums since: *One of the Boys* and *Teenage Dream*. Katy is often nominated for the same awards as Rihanna, but neither girl minds which one wins.

Rihanna and Katy have always looked out for one another when it comes to dating, and when Katy started to go out with British comedian and actor Russell Brand in September 2009, Rihanna wasn't too keen. She changed her mind, though, and was happy for two of them when they got engaged, three months later.

Rihanna confessed all to AOL when asked whether she thought Russell Brand was 'husband material' for Katy when she met him for the first time. She replied: 'He's funny. He's crazy. But it took a while for the penny to drop – "Duh! Russell and Katy are the perfect people for each other!" I first met him when he was interviewing me on TV. I was sick and it was the worst interview I have ever done. I was throwing up in a bucket and a doctor gave me a shot in my butt. Nothing was funny to me. Why am I talking to this idiot? He made me want to throw up again. This is a stupid interview. Then we did another interview

SARAH OLIVER

on MTV and I realised he was funny. I was probably a complete bitch, but only months afterwards did I get it.'

Rihanna was very excited about organising Katy's bachelorette party, and she thought Las Vegas was the perfect place to hold it. On 18 September 2010, RiRi and twenty or so of Katy's closest friends travelled to Las Vegas. They hung out in the VIP area of the Hard Rock Hotel's Beach Club pool, enjoying a bit of sunbathing while drinking champagne and beer, before the party started properly in the evening. Katy knew that Rihanna had planned a mad night, tweeting, 'Signing up for a liver transplant now.'

Once changed into their party minidresses, they all jumped into a huge Hummer and headed off to see the Cirque du Soleil perform their KÀ show. After being captivated by the skill of the acrobats, RiRi and Katy posed for photos with some of the performers, before moving on to the Italian restaurant Ago. The group then spent some time in the XS nightclub, before finishing the night in the Sapphire strip club.

Rihanna was glad that Katy had an amazing time, and admitted to Q Magazine: 'It was the first time I'd ever been in charge of a bachelorette party and it was a blast. We all flew to Las Vegas on a plane together, and went straight to the pool and drank. The goodie bags had a champagne glass and a hangover pill in them. Then we went to a Cirque du Soleil show, then to the strip club and to the tables for gambling.'

Days after returning from Las Vegas, she managed to

surprise her boyfriend Matt with a birthday party, held at a go-karting track in Los Angeles. She also attended another get-together for him at Drai's nightclub in Hollywood, on the night before his actual 26th birthday. Rihanna didn't look too happy as she was snapped going into the club, but that might have had more to do with the paparazzi hassling her than Matt. She wore an unusual black and white long-sleeved dress by designer Emilio Pucci.

Rihanna's next single was 'Only Girl (In the World)', and it was released in September 2010, two months before the album *Loud* came out. It was written by Stargate, Crystal Johnson and Sandy Vee, and was the lead track from *Loud*.

'Only Girl (In the World)' became Rihanna's ninth No. 1 in the US and also topped the charts in the UK, Ireland, Australia, Austria, Canada, Belgium, Poland, Germany, France, Italy, Romania, Hungary, Norway, New Zealand and Slovakia. It also won the Best Dance Recording award at the 2011 Grammys.

Rihanna admitted that she stretched herself for 'Only Girl (In the World)', and to make sure that she could get the big vocals right, she rested her voice on the days leading up to recording. She struggled with the insects and snakes in the areas where they filmed the video, but she knew the finished product would look beautiful.

The video was directed by Anthony Mandler, who has directed lots of Rihanna's videos, although he wasn't automatically appointed: he had to pitch for the job and went up against a few other top directors. Rihanna had sent them all some image and video references to give them an idea of what she wanted, and they then had to send her their story ideas for the video. When she looked through them, she felt that some of the concepts were too false and didn't work well, but she thought that Anthony's idea was spot-on. He had just picked out a mixture of nine old and new photos and sent them to her, and she knew that he understood what she was trying to achieve.

Rihanna told JustJared: 'It's really, really beautifully shot in these crazy, crazy, crazy places. We shot landscapes that we found a couple hours outside of L.A. It looks so unreal. It looks fake, like something out of a postcard with the beautiful hills. We had a lot of sunshine those couple of days, so it really worked with the whole essence of the video. But really, the video just shows this big landscape and the only person there is me.'

As well as having scenes of just Rihanna singing in beautiful landscapes, Anthony filmed her on a giant swing, lying in wild flowers and also surrounded by giant balloons.

Rihanna divulged to JustJared.com: 'We did this one really, really cool shot where they put me up [in harnesses]. I was suspended in the air on a swing that was just feet, feet, feet, feet high. It was crazy. They held me up on a crane, suspended in the air on top of a hill over a cliff. We just swung back and forth. It was *really* scary but it was fun!'

Fans loved seeing Rihanna looking so happy and carefree, and critics noted how girly it was, compared with the videos for her previous tracks, 'Hard' and 'Rockstar 101'.

When Katy Perry married Russell Brand on 23 October

2010 in a lavish ceremony in India, her best friend was nowhere to be seen. More than anything, Rihanna had wanted to be there, but she wasn't able to attend for a number of reasons. It is thought she spent the whole weekend stuck in a studio recording for her next album.

In the weeks that followed Rihanna was asked how it felt to miss Katy's big day and she would always reply honestly. She told Ryan Seacrest on LA's KIIS-FM: 'I will never, ever forgive myself for that – it was a crazy time, it was a crazy week, I'm switching management.

'There was no phone service in India and very little-to-no internet service, so it would have been a little irresponsible of me. I'm sad that I missed it.'

It is thought that she bought Katy and Russell a unique present worth thousands of pounds: an all-expenses paid trip to Tokyo!

The *Sun* reported that Rihanna's gift was two first-class tickets to Tokyo with four nights at the luxurious Mandarin Oriental hotel in a £1,500-a-night suite. She herself was keeping the present a secret and told reporters that her present was really cool but she was going to let Katy spill the beans, although it sounds like someone else beat her to it.

In the weeks that followed, Katy kept getting asked how she felt about Rihanna not being there, and she had to insist their friendship was still as strong as ever.

Katy told *Now* magazine: 'I was upset she couldn't make it, but let me promise you, there was no one more upset about it than her. When you have an album coming out, you don't have a spare second in the day and you're answerable to the record company.

'She felt really bad she couldn't be there, but we're still the very best of friends. My girl organised the best bachelorette party ever and I'll always love her to bits. It was just one of those really unfortunate things.'

After Katy and Russell tied the knot, lots of people started to ask when Rihanna and Matt would be walking down the aisle. Even Katy was trying to encourage her, as Rihanna explained to MTV: 'Katy thinks I should get married now, but she needs to calm down on that one. I mean, one day, but not just yet – we're having too much fun.'

She was also asked when she planned on having her own mini RiRis, but she doesn't know. 'I don't really plan on the age. It could be a year from now, it could be ten years from now. Whenever is right,' she explained to *Interview*. 'I mean, I have a lot of other stuff to accomplish before I get to kids. Whenever the time is right, I'll just know.'

In another interview she said she believes that a child 'deserves both parents.' She told *Interview* magazine: 'I'm just saying that whatever comes my way I'll be able to handle it, but in a perfect book, there would be marriage and kids.'

If she could, she'd love to bring up any children she has in the future in Barbados, but she knows that this won't be possible if she wants to remain a recording artist; she needs to live in the US. It is a shame, because if she lived in Barbados she would have her mum, her aunts and cousins on hand to help her. If she does have kids in the future, she probably will need nannies to help, because her family live so far away. Maybe having a family will encourage RiRi to slow down and take longer breaks between albums.

RiRi doesn't seem to have any preference as to whether her future kids are girls or boys, but she thinks that if she had a daughter, she'd probably end up with a rebellious one, to teach her a lesson after being a bit of a handful when she herself was growing up!

Just weeks after she missed out on Katy's wedding, Rihanna decided to create her own company called Rihanna Entertainment. Lots of big stars do this once they are established, so they can have more control and a bigger share of the profits. Rihanna's new company controls her music, movies, perfumes, future fashion lines, books, advertising and any other business venture she is involved in.

She also decided to change managers and would no longer be working with Marc Jordan and Rebel One Management. Instead, she would be managed by Jay-Z's Roc Nation Management. In a statement, she told The Associated Press that she was 'so excited to take this next step in my career.'

Fans had guessed this was on the cards, because she had said she was going to change management after she had to miss Katy and Russell's big day. Of course, she would never be able to get that occasion back, but at least this might stop something similar from happening in the future.

After settling into her new business role, Rihanna was

pleased with the progress she had made. While promoting *Loud*, she spoke to MTV about how she was feeling. There was, she said: 'A lot of growing up, a lot of responsibility in terms of taking control of my business and stuff like that.

'It feels so good, because the closer you are to your business, the clearer you are about a lot of things. And that responsibility doesn't feel like a burden. So I feel really good.'

In another interview with *USA Today*, she admitted that she had made sure she was 100 per cent ready to handle her own business affairs before she set up Rihanna Entertainment. She said: 'You can't have too much responsibility without being able to handle it in a responsible way, so I just waited until the time was right. It was now. Business is something I need to be a lot more serious about. I feel, like, really old doing it. It has made me grow up.'

She was also happy because of her relationship with Matt Kemp, and told *Marie Claire* magazine: 'I feel like I smile for real this time. The smiles come from inside, and it exudes in everything I do. People feel my energy is different. When I smile they can tell that it's pure bliss and not just a cover-up.

'The most important thing is to be happy and true to yourself. I don't want to look back at this 30 years from now and say, "I did it all to make them happy and I didn't enjoy it." I want to be able to say people loved me because of who I am.'

Rihanna seemed so happy with Matt that many fans had decided he must be the one for her, and expected them to announce their engagement someday soon, although the couple had only been dating for just under a year. Seeing Katy get married made Rihanna's fans want the same for her, but they had no idea that things weren't going to turn out as they planned.

YOU'RE SO AMAZING!

In October 2010, Rihanna decided to release 'What's My
Name?' featuring Drake. It went to No. 1 in the US, UK,
Brazil and Hungary, No. 3 in Ireland, Slovakia, New
Zealand and No. 4 in Norway. Rihanna and her
collaborator Drake actually had history as a couple.

Just weeks after she split up with Chris Brown in 2009,
the press had suggested Rihanna and Drake were dating,
after sources claimed to have seen them kissing and
cuddling at the Lucky Strike Lanes, a bowling alley in New
York. Rihanna got to know Drake after approaching him
to write a song for *Rated R*. In the end, his song didn't
make the final cut.

A year later Rihanna admitted that she was attracted to
Drake back then, but she wasn't ready because her
relationship with Chris had only just ended. In a radio

interview with Hot 97, she admitted: 'We weren't really sure what it was. We just went out – my friends, his friends. I definitely was attracted to Drake, but I think it is what it is, like it was what it was. We didn't want to take it any further. It was at a really fragile time in my life, so I just didn't want to get too serious with anything or anyone at that time.'

Drake seemed to take a different view on what happened between them, telling the *New York Post* in June 2010: 'I was a pawn. You know what she was doing to me? She was doing exactly what I've done to so many women throughout my life, which is show them quality time, then disappear. I was like, wow, this feels terrible.'

Rihanna was asked how she felt about being called a 'pawn' by Power 105.1 radio, and replied: 'I would definitely say that was wrong, he doesn't know what he's talking about. We just became friends and we left it at that. We get along really well. Drake has a youthful thing about him and he is very melodic with the way he writes, and I felt I needed someone like that for "What's My Name?"'

Things between them must now be fine, because if Drake had had a problem with RiRi they wouldn't have recorded the track together, and she would have asked someone else.

The video was directed by Philip Andelman in New York. Rihanna had never worked with him before, but she liked his ideas. She decided to go for the 'dancehall queen couture look' in this particular video; her street scenes were shot on 26 September 2010, and her scenes with Drake were shot a month later, on 27 October.

In the video, Rihanna goes to buy milk from a shop, but smiles when she sees Drake talking to the assistant. When he approaches her, she drops her milk carton on the floor. She's shown walking in Manhattan, getting close to Drake at home, drinking champagne with him, and later, dancing with friends at a night-time drumming party.

The video was filmed on the streets of New York, and so hundreds of people were watching, including the paparazzi. Someone recorded Rihanna doing her thing, and it was leaked online. This must have been disappointing for Rihanna but was probably inevitable, because it wasn't a closed set.

Since things didn't get too serious between Drake and RiRi, they were able to do 'What's My Name?' together. Rihanna was aware that the video might have upset Matt or made him feel uncomfortable, but she told the radio host: '[Matt] never said it out loud, but I don't know what he's thinking. He watched it the other day and he was like, "I love that video. It's a great video, babe." I don't know how true that really was, but he seemed to like it.'

It had actually been a bit weird for Rihanna to get so close to Drake when they first started shooting the video, but after a while she was able to relax and just get on with it. Having so many people around was also rather nerve-wracking for her, because she hadn't expected such a crowd to be there watching her do her scenes in the street; this was also difficult at first. She told BBC Radio 1: 'I just took a shot of a cocktail just before the video, then I went on the street and did my thing – there were a lot of people watching, so many cameras everywhere. I had to get in my own zone and do my thing.'

She also admitted in the interview that she was in love with Matt, saying: 'It's really difficult because we are so far from each other most of the year and we both have very demanding schedules. It gets difficult at times but it is what it is. I'm in love and I'm very happy, but we have only been dating for a few months so no wedding for now – we are taking it easy.'

After the video was completed she performed the song solo several times, including a performance on the US show *Saturday Night Live* and during *The X Factor* final in the UK. The first time she performed it with Drake was at the 2011 Grammy Awards in February of that year, and the second time was on her birthday, when she was performing at the NBA All Star Game.

Rihanna became involved in an augmented reality video concept for 'Doritos Late Night' in October 2010. She recorded the track 'Who's That Chick?' with David Guetta, and they filmed two versions of the video initially, one set in the day and another one at night. In order to see the night version of the video, fans had to buy a bag of Doritos Late Night chips, and use their smartphones or webcams to scan a barcode on the back of the bag, which allowed them to see the clip and change viewpoints by moving the bag. They could also switch between day and night.

Filming the two videos was strange for Rihanna, because

they had to be identical, so the same choreography was used and the same angles were shot: the only differences were the costumes and some aspects of the set.

A third video showing David Guetta on a spaceship and watching Rihanna on monitors was released in January 2011 (the Rihanna section of the video was taken from the earlier videos). The track was included on Guetta's album, *One More Love*, and was released for download on 22 November.

'Who's That Chick?' is a David Guetta track featuring Rihanna, not a Rihanna track featuring David Guetta, but UK radio stations kept saying that the track was on the *Loud* album when that was first released. As a consequence, David's management decided to write to all the radio stations to ask them to remove 'Who's That Chick?' from their playlists. Ultimately they wanted fans of the song to buy *One Love*, David's album, and not Rihanna's album. The track eventually reached No. 6 in the UK charts, but it may have done better had it been played on the radio more.

It charted at No. 1 in Slovakia and Belgium, No. 4 in Austria and Ireland, No. 5 in Norway, France, Finland and Spain and No. 6 in the UK, Germany and Holland. However, it fared less well in the US, as it only managed to reach No. 51. Indeed, Rihanna herself saw the song as more of a Doritos advert rather than a proper single.

During an interview with *Entertainment Weekly*, she was asked if she was hesitant about doing a song about being in a club, because so many songs seem to be about the same thing. She was really honest and said: 'Yeah, I know. And that's why it's a bonus track and not on *Loud*. It's a great song, but it's safe. It's like a lot of other songs out there.'

Her favourite version was the 'Day' one because she liked the brightness of it. It also reflected more of the new direction she was taking, as she was starting to add colourful items to her wardrobe. She was moving away from the darkness she had expressed in her 'Last Girl on Earth Tour'.

On Halloween 2010, Rihanna performed a Mad Hatter-themed version of 'Only Girl (In the World)' on the *X Factor Results Show*. For the performance she was shown sitting at a long table, enjoying a banquet with some glamorous guests and being served food by waiters. As she sang, she stood up, climbed on to the table and walked up and down it, while carrying on with her song. She then ate some cake before throwing it at one of the guests. This creates a huge food fight between the guests, and the song ends with Rihanna once again on the table.

The *X Factor* judges loved the performance, but host Dermot O'Leary felt it was a bit weird, as the guests continued to throw food at one another while he was interviewing Rihanna. He wanted them to stop, but she just said: 'It's fun, I want some. It tastes good!'

After she made her way off stage, the *X Factor* crew had just a few minutes to get the stage cleaned up during the advertising break. Sinitta was watching in the audience and tweeted: 'The stage is covered in cake, cream, cupcakes!!! Hahaha they are slipping all over trying to clean it up in time!! One minute to get the gunk off! I don't think they'll do it!'

After the show wrapped, RiRi was feeling hungry, so she headed off to a Japanese restaurant in Knightsbridge, then went on to the Whisky Mist nightclub.

SAYING
GOODBYE

Rihanna travelled to Barbados for the state funeral of Prime Minister David Thompson on 3 November 2010. As she made her way to the Kensington Oval she was applauded. Lots of people had said she wouldn't be there, but she had made the trip: she had to pay her respects. Ten thousand people attended the funeral, and it was screened on TV so that any Bajan who wanted to could watch. Rihanna cried during the service.

She released a short tribute, which was published on the website NationNews.com. In it she said: 'I am deeply saddened by the passing of Prime Minister David Thompson. He was a great man. True to form, even as he battled cancer, he remained focused on fulfilling his public responsibilities. This is a great loss to our country. My thoughts are with his family, who loved him dearly, his friends and with all of the citizens of Barbados.'

Having the opportunity to get to know David Thompson while he was alive, as well as other politicians on her home island, thanks to her role as the Youth and Cultural Ambassador for Barbados, has made Rihanna think about getting into politics. However, she did admit to a reporter from the *Sun* that she still has much to learn. She said: 'I'm not good at the politics side at the moment. It terrifies me because I am so young. But maybe one day in years, decades from now, I'll get involved. I think more pop stars should care about their country and how it's run.'

Rihanna's visit to Barbados was extremely short, because the next day she had to switch on the Christmas lights at the Westfield London Shopping Centre. It was only 4 November, so it was extremely early, but Rihanna did her best to get in the Christmas spirit. It must have been difficult mourning for her Prime Minister one day, then having to be all happy and excited the next day in front of hundreds of people.

She tweeted her fans: 'Westfield Mall, London! Its BANANAS in here! #RihannaNavy it doesn't get better than u guys.' When asked by presenter George Lamb what her Christmas wish was, she said 'more sleep', and told the hundreds of fans in the audience to add *Loud* to their wishlist before the big countdown.

'I just want to wish you all to get the gifts that you want!' she shouted.

The next night she had to be in Madrid to perform at the MTV EMA Awards Pre-Party, and so she didn't have much time to spare. Poor RiRi must have been worn out by all the travelling she had to do that week, but she kept on going and caught up on her sleep when she could.

She was invited to perform with Bon Jovi and couldn't believe that they wanted to sing with her. It didn't even sink in when they were on stage together, singing 'Livin' On A Prayer'; it was like a dream, and afterwards she tweeted her fans: 'Wait!…did I just rock out with Bon Jovi tonight??? WTFFFF!!!!!!!'

Jon Bon Jovi thought Rihanna did a great job, and he told the *Daily Star*: 'Rihanna was amazing. We didn't rehearse – she just came in for the soundcheck and nailed the song first time. I hear she's learning the guitar but who needs to play guitar when you can sing like that? It was so beautiful. She sang great, she's a sweetheart of a girl. She's a big fan, too. It was great!'

Bon Jovi probably didn't realise it, but that night on stage in the Teatro Circo Price was the highlight of Rihanna's year. 'Livin' On A Prayer' was one of her favourite songs, and so getting the opportunity to sing it with Bon Jovi was a dream come true. She had been listening to their music with her friends for years.

The actual MTV EMA Awards were held the next night, and although Rihanna didn't pick up any awards herself, she seemed happy as she performed 'Only Girl (In the World)' wearing a crown and nude corseted minidress. Katy Perry won the award for Best Video for 'California Gurls', so the friends had one award between them. Meanwhile, Lady Gaga picked up three awards: Best Female, Best Pop and Best Song for 'Bad Romance'.

After the awards ceremony finished, Rihanna and Katy headed for an Italian restaurant with Russell and Matt, no doubt to celebrate Katy's win and the fact that 'Only Girl (In the World)' was No. 1 in the UK, after knocking Cheryl Cole's 'Promise This' off the top spot. The girls certainly stood out from the other diners in the restaurant, as Rihanna wore a gorgeous blue sparkling Emilio Pucci minidress with an open back, and Katy was still wearing the green and silver dress with feather detailing that she wore to collect the award.

Rihanna's fifth album was called *Loud* and it came out on 12 November 2010. She had recorded it during her 'Last Girl on Earth Tour', between February and August. It was very different from *Rated R* as it was more up-tempo and dance-pop-based. Before the release, she told fans what to expect on her official fansite RihannaDaily.com: 'get LOUD everybody, get crazy, get excited, cuz I'm pumped. I'm just gonna be ME, cuz that's what u guys love the most, and that's what makes me feel best.

'Just being normal, normal for me is LOUD! Sassy, fun, flirty, energetic.'

One hundred of the best writers and producers were invited to write songs for *Loud,* and Rihanna could choose her favourites. The songwriters took part in big writing workshops in Miami and Los Angeles; Rihanna and her

209

team provided their ideas and the themes they wanted the songwriters to focus on.

On the day her *Loud* album came out RiRi felt as if it was her birthday, she was so excited. She had promotional interviews to do, but she was also thrilled that her brother Rorrey (who was 21) was flying in to see her.

She always buys a copy of her own albums, because she wants to experience what her fans experience. Rihanna loves going into a store, seeing it on the shelf and paying for it herself.

Most musicians would want to take a few months off after releasing an album and promoting it, but not Rihanna. She loves releasing albums in quick succession and doesn't see the point in stopping. A performer through and through, she wants to create great songs for her fans. She told *Good Morning America*: 'There's no rule that says you need to take a break between albums. We're here to make music and the fans want music.

'I feel like my fans can grow with me because it exudes the energy and place that I'm in at that moment, every time I make an album.'

Loud came out after 'Only Girl (In the World)' and 'What's My Name?' had already been released.

The graphic lyrics of 'Man Down' have caused some controversy, as Rihanna describes shooting a man dead in Central Station, but again there is another meaning behind them: she is singing about breaking someone's heart. She divulged: 'It's a very cleverly written song and what I love about it is that it's not a lyric you'd normally hear a female singing. The vibe is Jamaican and West Indian, that's something that's close to me.'

When asked about 'Man Down', RiRi explained to Q Magazine: 'It's an analogy. It's about breaking a certain man's heart. It's about ending his hopes and causing pain, which is like a gun shot.'

One of her favourite tracks on the album is the anthem 'Cheers', which cleverly samples Avil Lavigne's vocal from her ballad 'I'm With You'. It's one of the most catchy, feel-good songs on the album. She also liked the catchiness of 'What's My Name?'.

Rihanna was actually disappointed that she couldn't get Avril Lavigne to re-record the section of 'I'm With You' that she used in 'Cheers (Drink To That)'. She was about to make the request when she discovered that her producers had already embedded the original version in the track, and so it was too late. Even though she didn't manage to have Avril re-record it, you wouldn't have been able to tell any difference even if she had: it would have sounded virtually identical.

Rihanna told MTV: 'I'm just glad that we could use her sample, because it became such a huge part of the instrumental that if it were not in the song, it would change the whole vibe of it.'

'"Cheers" is one of my favourite songs. It makes you feel like celebrating. It gives you a great feeling inside, like you want to go out and have a drink. People can't wait for the weekend.'

During another interview, she revealed to *Entertainment*

Tonight: 'Loud is the word, the name of the album definitely reflects the attitude of it: it's really sassy and flirty, and it grabs your attention and that's why I enjoy it. It takes you through a really, really interesting ride. So colourful the album!'

She added that, for her, the most personal song on *Loud* was 'Fading' because, 'It's about the end of a relationship and how you deal with it and move on.'

To the BBC she said: 'I wanted to exude the energy and space I'm in right now – that's what I always try and do with my music. Right now in my life I feel very loud and in charge of my life, and I can't wait for everyone to hear the new album. It has such a variety of sounds, but it all makes sense for this album. There is a song on the album that is a straight-up Jamaican record and I love it – I even do a little chat on it at the end, haha.'

The album performed well, charting at No. 1 in the UK, Ireland, Croatia, Japan and Norway, No. 2 in Australia, Germany and Belgium and No. 3 in the US, Austria, France and Russia. Rihanna's songwriters, producers and collaborating artists included: Drake, Ne-Yo, Nicki Minaj, Taio Cruz, Sean Garrett, Alex da Kid, Timbaland, Rico Love, Ester Dean, David Guetta and Shontelle.

When *Loud* sold 10,000 fewer copies in the first week of its release in the US than *Rated R*, some people expected Rihanna to be worried, but she wasn't at all. She doesn't scare easily and she knew that one week of sales wasn't going to say whether the album was a hit or miss. Indeed, it might have sold just 170,000 copies that week, but 'Good

Girl Gone Bad' had only sold 160,000 in its first week, and it went on to sell millions!

When the album was released, the critics had mixed feelings about it. The *Los Angeles Times* and *USA Today* both gave it three out of four stars, but it only managed three out of five stars from *Rolling Stone* and *Slant* magazines. In his review for the *Boston Globe,* journalist James Reed described the album as 'an unabashed return to where Rihanna belongs: the dance floor. As if liberating herself from the depths, she's a force on these 11 songs, hop-scotching from electro-pop ('Only Girl (In the World)') to Top 40 balladry fit for Taylor Swift ('California King Bed')'. Metacritic gave the album a score of 67 out of 100, based on 22 reviews (this was slightly lower than *Rated R*, which had received a score of 76).

The tracks on the album were:

1. 'S & M'
2. 'What's My Name?' (featuring Drake)
3. 'Cheers (Drink to That)'
4. 'Fading'
5. 'Only Girl (In the World)'
6. 'California King Bed'
7. 'Man Down'
8. 'Raining Men' (featuring Nicki Minaj)
9. 'Complicated'
10. 'Skin'
11. 'Love the Way You Lie (Part II)' (featuring Eminem)

To launch *Loud* in the UK, Rihanna invited journalists to join her at a very special party in the West End. They sipped on cocktails as they listened to five songs, and then Rihanna talked about individual tracks and how she had wanted to create an album full of tracks that people would want to listen to, all the way through. She didn't want them to have to press the skip button.

Rihanna also held a special promotional day in Paris, to get people excited about the release of *Loud*. As well as giving interviews she performed as well, singing 'Only Girl (In the World)' on the French TV show, *Le Grand Journal*, on a stage covered in white balloons. After the performance, she was being interviewed when the female host ran up to the stage and started to perform her own version of 'Only Girl (In the World)' with two backing dancers! Rihanna laughed because it was so funny, but the next minute the entire audience got up, walked over to the stage and joined in. It must have been a very surreal moment for RiRi.

During her whistlestop tour of Paris, she did manage to go shopping with her friends in a Prada store, and had a quick look at a display of sneakers. She also visited the Jean Paul Gaultier fashion house with Matt Kemp and her entourage, and was snapped having dinner at the Sardana A Tavola restaurant.

The cover art chosen for the *Loud* album was a close-up of Rihanna's face and the top of one of her shoulders. She has her eyes closed and her mouth is slightly open. Her lips are painted bright red and her red hair frames the shot. You can just about make out part of the 'rebelle fleur' tattoo on her neck. This was the first of Rihanna's album covers not to have her name on the front, and simply said 'L O U D' at the bottom. In many ways, this shows just how much she has achieved since *Music of the Sun* came out in 2005. She is so well known now that she doesn't need her name on the cover to tell people whose album it is: they know immediately, as soon as they see her face.

The 'Only Girl (In the World)' cover art was the first cover fans saw from the *Loud* group, because the album had not yet been released. It was the crossover single from 'Rated R' to 'Loud', which may explain why Rihanna continued the semi-nude theme of some of the *Rated R* singles' cover art. In the 'Only Girl (In the World)' cover art, she kneels naked in a field, holding a red dress up against her body. Her hip tattoo is clearly visible and she wears a necklace and an armlet. Her hair is wild and free, a theme running through the other *Loud* single covers. Rihanna's name is missing, and just the softer 'R' logo is displayed in the top left-hand corner, with the song title at the bottom of the image.

For the 'What's My Name?' cover art, Rihanna chose a beautiful image that makes her look almost like a bridesmaid. She wears her hair loose, with a jewelled flower headband, and the only glimpse of the outfit we see is some peach-coloured netting. There is a blue hue to the image, as there is in the cover art for the other *Loud* singles; the background is a peach colour, which seems almost like sunlight shining down on Rihanna as it covers part of her hair. The softer 'R' logo is in the top left-hand side, while the title of the track and the credit stating Drake is featured on it are found at the bottom of the image.

The cover art for 'S & M' was very different from the single's video: it was a blurry shot of Rihanna leaning forward, her red hair unkempt, and with large wooden beaded necklaces around her neck. She looks downwards and the image has a blue hue to it. Her make-up is very natural, and at the bottom left-hand side is the softer 'R' logo and her name. On the bottom right-hand side, 'S & M' is in a handwritten-style script.

For 'Man Down', Rihanna chose a black and white shot of her face. She has two fingers to her lips, with an oversized flower ring on her left hand, and large sunglasses hiding her eyes. The single's title is in a tattoo-like script on the right hand side of the image, alongside her name.

The cover art for 'California King Bed' shows RiRi sitting down, wearing a cream dress and biting on an oversized necklace. She is looking at someone or something off-camera. It is a soft and romantic shot, with the single's title in the bottom left-hand corner. Her R logo is at the top left.

A few days after *Loud* was released, RiRi had gone out for a meal with people from her label in New York, and Justin Bieber had been there. RiRi tweeted: 'Justin Bieber just flashed me his abs in the middle of a restaurant! Wow! He actually had a lil 6 pack! Sexy, lol! #Beliebersplzdontkillme'

She had been chatting to Justin when she asked him if he had abs, and when he told her that he did, she made him show her. After Rihanna tweeted her message, Justin tweeted: 'Great night out to dinner with the beautiful @rihanna... I'm not complaining... RiRi....check for the new album.'

In the past he has said that he's asked RiRi out on a date, but she turned him down because he's too young for her. She still likes him, though, and when asked in an interview who she liked best, Justin Bieber or the Jonas Brothers, she replied: 'Justin!'

After enjoying her meal with Justin and the others, RiRi had to work really hard for a few days before her big performance at the American Music Awards on 21 November 2010. She was given the task of opening the show and did so in style, belting out an a capella version of 'Love The Way You Lie Part II' from a tree and then 'falling' off, before reappearing to sing 'What's My Name?' and 'Only Girl (In the World)'. Rihanna started off by performing on her own, and commanded the audience's full attention as she danced and sang, before being joined by her own dancers and drummers. It was a slick performance, showing everyone watching that she was without doubt one of the best performers in the world. Quite rightly, the audience, which included Beyoncé, Justin Bieber, Usher, Katy Perry, Pink and many more top artists and people associated with the record business, all gave her a standing ovation.

Later on that night she was named Favourite Soul/R&B Female Artist, beating Alicia Keys and Sade. She was presented with the trophy on stage by Nicki Minaj, Taio

Cruz and Trey Songz. She thanked her fans, L.A. Reid, Def Jam, Roc Nation and her crew for their support, before slapping Nicki's backside as they exited the stage!

CONTROVERSY

Rihanna returned to *The X Factor* in December 2010, this time to duet with Matt Cardle in the final. Each of the finalists had to do a duet, and Matt was thrilled to get the chance to perform 'Unfaithful' with Rihanna. After they sang, she told the audience: 'He's amazing, he's adorable and I'm honoured to share the stage with him. I really love your work – I wish you all the best. He is going to go very far!'

Rihanna and Matt's duet was by far the best of the night, with their chemistry clear to see. Rebecca Ferguson sang 'Beautiful' with Christina Aguilera, One Direction sang 'She's The One'with Robbie Williams, while Cher Lloyd did a mash-up of 'Where Is The Love' and 'I Gotta Feeling' with Will.i.am.

After the duets, Rihanna took to the stage later on to perform her track 'What's My Name?' and Christina Aguilera performed 'Express' from her latest movie, *Burlesque*. Over 2,000 people ended up complaining about the performances, though, because they didn't think they were suitable for children watching at home.

Later that night, Matt was crowned winner of *The X Factor* 2010, but he had one regret: he wishes he had kissed RiRi during their duet. That night he released his winner's song, 'When We Collide', and it sold 439,000 copies in the first week alone, making it the UK's Christmas No. 1.

In April 2011, the media regulator Ofcom ruled that Rihanna's and Christina Aguilera's performances did not breach broadcasting rules and were 'at the limit' of acceptability for a pre-9 o'clock broadcast.

Rihanna spent Christmas 2010 in Barbados with her family and friends. She was heading home, when she got a big surprise at the airport: her family had travelled all the way to Miami so that she wouldn't have to travel back to Barbados on her own! She was totally shocked when she arrived at the departure gate, and later tweeted: 'I'm in Miami Airport...Guess who just popped up and surprised me at my Gate??? My mooooommmyyyyy...and my AUNTY!!! We all going home together... #BarbadosIloveyou'

Once they all landed, RiRi headed off for a party her brother Rorrey was hosting, and enjoyed being Robyn Fenty again, just a Bajan girl. She had a really relaxing holiday, catching up with people she hadn't seen in a long time. Two days before Christmas, she decided to visit her mum's fashion store in the Decosta Mall. As soon as people spotted her, the news spread that Rihanna was heading for the 'Fabulous Boutique'. One fan rushed there and spotted RiRi standing with her mom, her friends and the people working at the store. She bought a T-shirt, and then asked Monica if she could meet Rihanna. RiRi was happy to pose for a photo, and the fan left feeling as if she was on Cloud Nine.

Rihanna enjoyed a private Christmas Day with her family, but was spotted on Sandy Lane beach the next day with her friends: she wanted to make the most of being near the sea, and Sandy Lane beach is one of the finest on the West Coast of Barbados. It is one of the best places to go swimming because the water is so calm, and lots of people enjoy using jet skis there. She spent the next few days on the beach, catching up with friends and having fun. Her bodyguard, Sonya and Ja'Maal Buster joined her on the beach along with her brother Rajad. Ja'Maal is the man behind RiRi's gorgeous eyelashes and goes by the nickname 'The Eyelash Guru'.

In the evenings they would go somewhere for drinks, and one night they headed to the Pre-Old Year's Models & Bottles party at the Ship Inn Club. The Models & Bottles party is held every Tuesday night, and is the biggest party night in Barbados, with 1,000 people turning up each week. On an average night they serve 400 bottles to partygoers, and the Pre-Old Year's party was the final Models & Bottles party of the year.

RiRi hadn't been particularly close to her father for two years when the media reported that she had decided to forgive him for the things he had done in the past that upset her. She has always maintained a relationship with him, even when he was on drugs and had split up with her mum, but when he got drunk on her tour bus during a visit, she decided enough was enough. She was even more hurt when he spoke to the media about her attack without first discussing this with her.

In one interview she talked frankly to *Vogue* about her relationship with her father, and how she's been left feeling stunned each time he has sold stories to the press or given them photos of herself as a child. She never expected him to do something like that, because she thought he would be loyal to her, and wasn't the kind of man to want to profit from her fame by selling stories about her. Furthermore, she was deeply hurt when he spoke to the press shortly after her attack.

Rihanna explained to the fashion magazine interviewer: 'My dad went to the press and just told them a bunch of lies because he hadn't talked to me after that whole thing. He never called to find out how I was doing, if I was alive, nothing. He just never called. He went straight to the press and got a cheque.'

In the last few months of 2010, RiRi seemed to have decided to let Ronald back into her life. She went to see him more and even visited him on Christmas Day; she treated him to some new clothes and aftershave, and they seem to be mending their relationship. The *Mirror* interviewed him a few weeks later, and he confessed: 'Maybe we're not as close as we were when she was growing up here and was at school. But we are blood, we do not stay angry and we are friends again.'

He also talked about the incident that caused their rift two years earlier: 'We did have a disagreement about the drinking on the tour. I got plastered on the tour bus. I can drink rum or beer, but vodka does not like me – or gin. She blasted me for that – she was always lippy, from her small days. I was picked up from the hotel in the morning and I was just shuttled to the airport.'

Rihanna will never decide not to love her father. After all, she wouldn't have been able to handle some of the things that have come her way if she hadn't been made a stronger person by what she went through as a child. She thinks her childhood gave her a thick skin, and helped her deal with the sometimes brutal recording industry. Her life might be like a huge rollercoaster at times, but she always has more ups than downs.

Interviewers like to talk about her parents splitting up or her dad's drug problems, and paint the picture that RiRi's childhood was horrible, but things weren't so black and white. Yes, she witnessed some terrible scenes, but at the same time she had fantastic days on the beach with her family and friends; she also learned how to swim with the help of her father. She can remember practising how to write with him as well. He wasn't the hopeless father that the media like to portray: when he wasn't on drugs, he was great.

Now, as an adult, RiRi tries just to focus on the positive experiences she had with her father while growing up, and tries to forget all the bad times. Thinking of them won't change anything and her whole family have learned to move on.

On 28 December 2010, the news broke that Rihanna had split with Matt Kemp. The media reported that the split was down to the singer's schedule being so busy, and that the couple had struggled to see each other. Matt's schedule was pretty packed, too, as he had to travel whenever the Dodgers had away games.

RiRi has always been honest with her fans, and in an interview with BBC 1Xtra back in October 2010, she admitted that things were tough, saying: 'It's really difficult because we are so far from each other most of the year, and we both have very demanding schedules. It gets difficult at times, but it is what it is.'

Rihanna saw in the New Year in Las Vegas, hosting a party at the Pure Nightclub inside Caesar's Palace. She wore a gorgeous red maxidress with sheer stripes by designer Louise Goldin and seemed happy as she chatted to guests. After doing her duty at that party, she moved on to The Cosmopolitan party, hosted by Jay-Z. The Cosmopolitan is a $3.9 billion hotel (approximately £2.3 billion). RiRi changed out of the red dress and put on a brown wraparound dress, before dancing the night away with Beyoncé, Kanye West, Jennifer Lopez, Gwyneth Paltrow and Chris Martin in the hotel's Marquee Nightclub.

It was a night of singing and laughter: Beyoncé performing 'Forever Young' with Chris Martin, John Mayer performing '99 Problems' with Jay-Z, Kanye performing 'Runaway', 'Homecoming' and 'Monster' with Jay-Z (as well as being DJ) and RiRi performing 'What's My Name?'.

There was so much champagne on offer that people were dancing with a bottle each, and at $300 (£180) a time, the Armand de Brignac champagne bill must have run into thousands. Rihanna might have had a nice time the year before – ringing in the New Year with Matt in Abu Dhabi – but to be surrounded by Jay-Z and her celebrity friends, who have become like family to her, must have been truly amazing! It's just a shame that Katy Perry and Russell Brand weren't there to celebrate with her, too.

2011 NEW YEAR, NEW AWARDS

A few days after her New Year celebration, RiRi won three awards at the People's Choice Awards: Favourite Pop Artist, Favourite Music Video and Favourite Song (both for 'Love The Way You Lie'). Eminem picked up another two in addition to the two he shared with RiRi: Favourite Hip-Hop Artist and Favourite Male Artist. Sadly RiRi and Eminem were both too busy to make it to the awards ceremony in person.

2011 was turning out to be a great year for Rihanna, as *Loud* became the world's top-selling album for two consecutive weeks, and she was named the first female solo artist to achieve five No. 1 singles in five consecutive years in the UK. The only male artist to achieve the same feat was Elvis Presley, back in the 1950s.

RiRi was actually No. 1 in both the single and album

charts in the UK on Sunday, 9 January 2011, as 'What's My Name?' moved up a place and knocked Matt Cardle off the top spot. 'Only Girl (In the World)' was at No. 9, and her collaboration with David Guetta, 'Who's That Chick?', was at No. 10. She had previously reached No. 1 simultaneously in the single and album charts back in 2007, when 'Good Girl Gone Bad' topped the album chart and 'Umbrella' topped the singles chart.

RiRi was so happy that she tweeted this message to her UK fans: 'Another week! LOUD and What's My Name are the #1 ALBUM and SINGLE respectively!!! UK you are on FYAH!!!Rah Rah! THANK U! Where my #UKNavy'

NICKI AND KANYE

Nicki Minaj is a rapper and singer-songwriter originally from Trinidad, who was brought up in New York. She collaborated with Rihanna on the track 'Raining Men' for RiRi's album *Loud*, and then Rihanna returned the favour by collaborating on 'Fly' for Nicki's first studio album, *Pink Friday*. Nicki has become a good friend of Rihanna's, and for a while the media speculated that the two women were dating after Nicki told E! News in early January: 'We're shooting the video with Rihanna for "Fly" this weekend. We're going to save the world in more ways than one with the video and that's all I can say about that. I love RiRi! I mean, when she's not grabbing my ass, she's a sweet girl.'

The girls enjoyed messing around and when they filmed the video for 'Fly' they just had fun with their tweets. Rihanna tweeted a photo of them together, with Nicki sticking out her tongue and RiRi pouting, and the message: 'Me and Nikki in our new crib, lol! Gettin busy on set of FLY!!! It's so hard to keep my hands off!'

Nicki joined in and replied: 'Lol. If we're gonna liv 2gthr and hook up u gotta learn how 2 spell my name! Lmaooooooo'

Rihanna then fired back: 'b**ch don't u hear me askin what my OWN name is??? Lol! My bad, I'll make it up to u *wink*'

The two thought it was hilarious that people believed that they were living together because of that one photo and a few tweets. Neither girl could have expected that they would become such good friends in a short period of time, even though Nicki had wanted to work with RiRi for quite a while. She wrote on her Facebook page: '"Fly" is one of my absolute faves. I wanted to work with Rihanna for a long time. I'm very proud of her accomplishments, especially since she was born on an island like me.

'This song is a female empowerment song. But then again, it's not specific to just women. It speaks about flying, soaring high in the face of every single solitary adversity that comes your way.

'I speak about how the media has attempted to box me in and how that has made me feel suffocated. After years of being dragged thru the mud, I've mustered up the courage to re-define myself. I believe that I represent an entire generation. My fans have become my family, and together we have become a movement. Get ready for it. We came to win.'

Nicki originally planned to release 'Fly' in April/May 2011, but she decided to release her track 'Super Bass' instead, because both she and Rihanna had quite a few singles they wanted to push from their respective albums. *Pink Friday* came out only seven days after *Loud,* and Nicki therefore felt that postponing the release of 'Fly' would be for the best.

She explained to MTV, back in March 2011: 'I'm gonna hold off on the Rihanna video and the Rihanna single for a little bit longer, 'cause we both kind of dropped at the same time. So she has a lot of [songs] in rotation and I want to let her stuff have a moment and do its thing, dominate radio. [Instead], I wanted to come out with something more fun.'

Kanye West values Rihanna both as an artist and a friend, so when he made a rough copy of his album, *My Beautiful Dark Twisted Fantasy*, he let RiRi listen to it. Immediately, she picked out 'All Of The Lights' as her favourite, and when he offered to let her appear on the track, she just had to say 'yes', even though he wanted to record it at 2am!

Rihanna sang the song's hook and was joined on the single by Alicia Keys, Elton John, Fergie, John Legend, Elly Jackson, Charlie Wilson, Ryan Leslie, The-Dream, Tony Williams and Kid Cudi. Only Kanye, Rihanna and Kid Cudi appear in the actual video.

It is clear which parts of the single Rihanna sings, but for many of the other artists it is not so obvious, as Kanye layered up their vocals. Elly Jackson told MTV: 'He just basically wanted to use his favourite vocalists from around the world to create this really unique vocal texture on his record, but it's not the kind of thing where you can pick it out. I don't have a verse or anything. I can't actually hear my voice on it, but apparently it's there!'

'All Of The Lights' was released on 18 January 2011, and three weeks later, the video premiered on 19 February. Initially it was removed from YouTube for a time over safety fears because of the flashing lights and colours in the video, but it was later reinstated with the warning: 'This video has been identified by Epilepsy Action to potentially trigger seizures for people with photosensitive epilepsy. Viewer discretion is advised'.

The song reached No. 19 in the US charts and No. 15 in the UK charts. It did best in Belgium, where it was No. 3, in Australia, where it got to No. 8, and in Ireland and New Zealand, where it was No. 13.

On 31 January 2010, Rihanna picked up another Grammy award, this time for her collaboration with Jay-Z and Kanye West. Winning a Grammy for 'Run This Town' made her very happy; she was grateful that Jay-Z and Kanye had picked her to sing it with them, because at the end of the day they could have chosen Beyoncé or any other female artist.

Rihanna has worked on many collaborations over the years. She has worked with Eminem, Akon, Sean Paul, Jay-Z, Kanye West... and many more top artists. Lots of her collaborations have gone straight to the top of the charts, and she's picked up numerous MTV and Grammy Awards.

Rihanna is such a big star that other singers can

sometimes get starstruck by her, but she is looking forward to the new collaborations she will be recording in the near future.

Cheryl Cole probably never expected Rihanna would want to sing a duet with her, but after meeting the *X Factor* judge in person and hearing the type of music she was releasing, RiRi was certainly interested. She thought Cheryl is a beautiful woman with a beautiful voice.

They share a mutual friend who told Rihanna that Cheryl would love to record something with her, after Rihanna said the same thing about wanting to work with Cheryl while she was waiting in the dressing room before one of her *X Factor* performances. The friend passed on Rihanna's mobile number to Cheryl, so they could have a chat about what they might do together.

Cheryl must have been really glad that the friend decided to help make the duet happen. She told MTV: 'I couldn't believe it when I heard Rihanna wanted to work with me. When I found out she wanted to collaborate, I got goose bumps all over.

'We're definitely doing something together next year [2011]. I'm totally up for it!'

In April 2011, the website M is for Music stated that an insider had told them: 'Cheryl's management want her to become the next big popstar in America and are working on securing some A-List names for the album.

'A Rihanna duet is a certainty and Will.i.am is trying to convince Minaj to work on the LP, too. Katy Perry has also been in talks with Cheryl about a duet, as she is a big fan.'

UK Rihanna fans might be looking forward to seeing the collaboration between RiRi and Cheryl, but the majority of RiRi's fans want to see her duet with Katy Perry first. This would be the best collaboration RiRi has ever done (not to put down those with Jay-Z, Kanye or Eminem). When RiRi and Katy finally get the chance to record a track together, the song will be something people won't expect, because they don't want it to be predictable: it will be a fun track and something catchy, perhaps the best track either of them has ever done.

They both admire each other's work, and Katy even included her own acoustic version of 'Only Girl (In the World)' to her set list on tour. She sang it as part of a medley with Jay-Z's 'Big Pimpin' and Willow Smith's 'Whip My Hair'.

It seems like everyone wants to do a duet with Rihanna, even Susan Doyle. The *Britain's Got Talent* runner-up was being interviewed by the *Sun* newspaper when she said she wasn't sure whether she'd be good at R&B, but she could dye her hair purple and do a track with Rihanna.

When RiRi found out, she tweeted: 'Hold up! I might be a lil late, but just heard that THEE SuBo wants to collab wit ME??!? I'm game, doesn't get much cooler than this. #BOOM.'

She obviously didn't mind that Susan's *The Gift* album had stopped *Loud* from taking the No. 1 spot in the US album charts.

Even 'DJ Got Us Fallin' In Love' singer Usher wanted to collaborate with Rihanna. When interviewed on the *Loose*

Women TV show, he said: 'Of course I'd do a track with her. We've been friends and our teams work together, and we've talked about working together in the past, but it could potentially happen.

'I would love to work with her: I think she's an incredible artist.'

RIHANNA FIGHTS BACK AGAINST THE BULLIES

When we think of Rihanna, we think about a confident woman, commanding the stage and never afraid, but this isn't the real Rihanna. She discussed the fact that she thinks she's misunderstood with Kanye West, when he asked her questions for *Interview* magazine. She told him: 'They only see the tough, defensive, aggressive side, but every woman is vulnerable – they have vulnerability. So of course I'm going to have that side. It's not a major part of who I am, but it's definitely there. I just don't like people to see me cry.'

When interviewed on the Ed Lover Radio Show, Rihanna decided to hit back at bloggers who write horrible things about her and other celebrities. She was quite naïve when she first started to read blogs, but now she is more cynical. She said: 'I still read the blogs sometimes –

it depends on what it is I am trying to find out. I'm a lot more numb to it now, only because I understand what it is: it's a community for people who don't have anything else to do and hate themselves.

'They hate their life, they hate their job, they hate their appearance, they are uncomfortable with who they are, so what makes them feel good is talking smack about other people who they think they will never ever see in their life, and they happen to be celebrities.'

Obviously Rihanna isn't talking about all bloggers, just the ones who think it's clever to write nasty things about people they don't even know. She thinks they wouldn't be quite so brave if they had to meet the celebrities they write about face-to-face, instead of hiding behind their computer screens.

As well as being bullied by bloggers, RiRi has had to face bullying behaviour from the press and paparazzi, who seem to enjoy making things up about her to make her look bad or twisting the truth. RiRi was criticised after having her photo taken with some kids while wearing a 'F★★★ You' necklace, but she couldn't help it: she had just come out of a restaurant when she was asked by the young girls if she would mind having a photograph taken with them. She never turns down her fans, and so she said 'yes', not realising the backlash she would face. If she had said 'no', then the girls would have been upset, and the press would probably have released a story saying how heartless Rihanna was and that she snubs her fans. Sometimes she just can't win. The writing on the necklace is so small that the girls more than likely wouldn't have noticed it anyway.

As far as RiRi is concerned, the worst things that the media and bloggers have ever written about her was when they talked about a scar she has on her lip, and blamed it on an STD. They suggested that Chris Brown attacked her because he thought it was a cold sore, caused by herpes. Rihanna told Q *Magazine*: 'It's not true, it's a f****** scar. On my lip. That's there every day of my life.'

Rihanna will never let the bullies win, and always maintains her composure. She has worked too hard to let anyone ruin her dream. She is a fighter!

S & M

Rihanna's fourth single released from *Loud* was 'S & M', and it first came out on 21 January 2011. It was written by Stargate, Corey Jackson Carter, Ester Dean and Sandy Wilhelm, and was a dance-pop track. An 'S & M Remix' was released on 11 April, with Britney Spears collaborating on the track (of which, more later).

Originally Rihanna had considered releasing 'Cheers (Drink to That)' as the fourth single, but she decided that 'S & M' would be the track fans really wanted her to release. The fans had liked how controversial it was, and when they saw the video they were amazed. Director Melina Matsoukas and Rihanna (who was co-directing) created a work so risqué that it was actually banned in 11 countries! After labelling the video 'inappropriate', YouTube wouldn't permit anyone under 18 to view it.

Rihanna found this strange and tweeted: 'They watched 'Umbrella'. I was full nude.'

When the BBC heard that RiRi's single was called 'S & M' they decided to rename it and started calling it 'Come On'. This didn't please Rihanna one bit: she hated the fact that they had wiped out the name and some of the lyrics from her song, in order to make it more 'suitable'.

'S & M' might have some raunchy lyrics, but as Rihanna explained to Spin.com, the line, 'Sticks and stones may break my bones, but chains and whips excite me,' isn't just about sex. She revealed: 'I don't think of it in a sexual way, I'm thinking metaphorically. It's more of a thing to say that people can talk. People are going to talk about you, you can't stop that – you just have to be that strong person and know who you are so that stuff just bounces off. And I thought it was super bad-ass.'

Melina Matsoukas admitted to MTV: 'When I go out to make something, I kind of go out with the intention to get it banned – well, not to get it banned, I always want my stuff played – but to make something provocative. So when you do something that's provocative, there's usually a repercussion. It's gonna be talked about, or banned or slandered in some way, but it's making an effect and people are having a dialogue about it, so to me, that's successful.'

She felt that the video's content fits with the theme of the title, and believed that YouTube's banning it for under-18s wouldn't stop the fans seeing it if they wanted.

Rihanna also told MTV what she loved about the track when she heard the demo for the first time. She said: 'I love that song. When I first heard it, it was a demo and it was rough and some of it was done, but I knew, I knew what it was the minute I heard it. And the energy in that song is so rebellious and in your face, unapologetic and that's what I loved about it.

There was no turning back from that song and the lyrics really make sense to the way I feel, and it's a metaphorical song, y'know it's really not about sex. It's not about anything S&M, but we play off of that.'

RiRi told *Extra*: '"S & M" is my favourite video I've ever done, and I can't wait to keep making more incredible videos and beating them out every time. "S & M" is going to be a hard one to beat.'

In fact, 'S & M' was RiRi's eighteenth Top 10 hit in the US.

The critics were split when it came to writing their reviews. Several felt it was a track that would have been better suited to the *Rated R* album, while others believed it was a great dance-pop song and very sexy, too. The song performed well, staying at No. 3 in the UK charts for three consecutive weeks. In Australia it did even better, charting at No. 1 for two weeks. When the Britney Spears version was released, it gave Rihanna another Top 10 single in the US, her tenth USA No. 1, and No. 1 in Canada.

Celebrity blogger Perez Hilton will never forget the moment he was asked to be in the video, and admits the appearance is one of his career highlights. During an interview, he told MTV: 'My takeaway from this video was that it was very strategically made to get attention and make a point. It reminded me of Madonna during the "Erotica" phase and the "Hollywood"/ "American Life" phase, both of which were controversial.'

He liked the message behind the song and video, and added: 'What I love especially was that you got to see Rihanna in a new light. We've never seen Rihanna like this before, plus it wasn't too serious, and that's a great message: You shouldn't let what others say about you affect you.

'She's being all sorts of crazy in the video and it's like she's saying, "Be who you are and let your freak flag fly". I'm really emboldened and inspired by the message of "S & M" and the movement that seems to be happening. Pop songs can be meaningful songs.'

Filming the video wasn't all plain sailing for RiRi, though, because she had to keep eating bananas all day, and she told her fans via Twitter: 'I HATE bananas too, I made 'em gimme a spit bucket in between takes.

'I am really happy rt now abt the tremendous response from everyone on the S&M clip... glad u love the smell it!

'I had tons of fun in the pink zebra room! My bff M, Perez, Trannys, a hott little person and a silver fox! Can't be crazier.'

When celebrated photographer David LaChapelle saw 'S & M' he was not impressed. He felt that a lot of the imagery in the video was 'directly derived from and substantially similar' to his work. In February 2011, the *Daily Mail* and various other newspapers and magazines reported that LaChapelle was suing for unspecified damages.

When RiRi was invited to release her own perfume line, she spent time thinking about it. She has never been one for doing things just to make money, and she didn't want to put her name on something she hadn't created herself. Since she was a little girl, she has always loved perfume, and she knew the fans had been waiting a long time for her to release a fragrance or two.

She decided that the time was right, and set about creating the perfume with an expert team of perfume designers. Her first fragrance was released on 26 January 2010, and it was available in the Macy's chain of department stores to begin with, before going on sale in other outlets in the US and beyond.

Because releasing a perfume was something that Rihanna had wanted to do for a long time, she was keen to give it a name that meant something special to her and her family. She chose the name 'Reb'l Fleur', a nickname her grandmother gave her when she was a little girl. She would say Rihanna was her 'Rebel Flower', and that is why she decided to have this tattooed on her neck. On her neck it is spelled differently as 'Rebelle Fleur', and some people have suggested that it should be 'Fleur Rebelle' instead, because the French usually put the adjectives after the nouns they follow. This wouldn't be appropriate, though, because her grandmother never called her 'Fleur Rebelle'.

Before her perfume hit the shelves, she talked to *People* magazine about the challenge of finding a unique scent. She said: 'Over the years, I layered many different scents to get something that was truly my own, but I wanted something that said, "Rihanna was here" – something delicious and special, a fragrance with subtle hints that linger and leave a sexy memory.'

A lot of money was spent creating the online video for Reb'l Fleur, because the people behind the perfume wanted to create a buzz about it, rather than sticking to the normal magazine ads that are used to push other celebrity perfumes. Indeed, the total advertising budget behind the launch was estimated to be $5 million.

The video for the perfume shows two sides of RiRi: there is the good Rihanna wearing a peach dress, and on the other side of the mirror the bad Rihanna is in a black minidress. As she steps through the mirror, she changes outfits and personalities. Fans watching the video have the ability to make RiRi switch sides, which makes this perfume ad video so unique. It's no wonder that it went viral. Fans rushed out to buy it, and it immediately became the No. 1 bestselling perfume in the US, a fantastic achievement.

The video was produced by Droga5, an award-winning advertisement agency. They had Rihanna walk backwards for some sections of the video, rather than doing this artificially, because they wanted viewers not to realise which way they had filmed it. Even the music was composed with this in mind; whichever way the video was played the music was the same, because Droga5 had wanted it be 'palindromic', so the notes for each frame are identical.

Earlier predictions were that the video would be viewed

worldwide more than 20 million times, but it looks as if it could do even better. Once the fans got to try the fragrance for themselves, they realised it was just as good as the video.

The perfume was produced by Parlux Fragrances Inc., who have also produced fragrances for Paris Hilton, Jessica Simpson and Queen Latifah. RiRi was fully involved in the process of creating the perfume, and would have meetings with the designers to discuss what she wanted it to smell like, as well as the bottle and packaging design. The finished scent was based on the perfumes RiRa combined herself so she smelled unique, and was created by Marypierre Julien and Caroline Sabas. They chose a bottle shaped like a stiletto, which reflects how RiRi wanted the perfume to be: 'Like high heels with a short, flirty dress.'

Perfume experts loved Reb'l Fleur, with Marie-Helene Wagner writing on The Scented Salamander blog: 'Just like Rihanna may lead you on a red herring trail with her neon raspberry-dyed hair, showy behavior and mega-wattage stage-diva persona, the perfume finally lets through a much more subtle personality, one which is even classical in a sense, more like the Fleur (flower) part in her affectionate *petit nom* "Rebelle Fleur."

'The fragrance may seem almost bipolar, with its juxtaposition of garisher notes on a harder-to-detect discreet aroma of classicism. But it offers this very positive, intangible quality in perfumery, which is that the more you smell the perfume (on skin, please), the more you like it and appreciate it, discovering each time new hidden nuances and qualities.

'The first part may well send you the message that if you

don't identify with a girly, flaming red singer, then there isn't much left for you to smell. But if you persist, then there is an anchoring of the scent which is extremely classic, light, restrained, lady-like and soft. You start with a color-saturated Hawaiian shirt and you end up almost with a convent sister's shirt, starched and clean as she is taking a walk by the breezy sea.'

When RiRi launched the perfume in Macy's department stores in the US, hundreds of fans would turn up to see her and get their hands on a bottle of Reb'l Fleur each time.

Before she arrived at one of the launches, she tweeted: 'I hope yall lookin REAL sexy @ Macy's rt now! Mama's on her way, and she smellin real good too.'

At another launch, Muriel Gonzalez from Macy's told the press: 'This scent really strikes a chord with her fans. They love the contrast of hard and soft elements – the rebel and the fleur.' Fred Purches of Parlux Fragrances added: 'Rihanna brings a lot of energy and a lot of people. It boosts sales, but it's also about the resonance afterwards.'

FORGIVENESS

In February 2011 Rihanna's lawyer Donald Etra told E! News that she has agreed that the restraining order stopping Chris Brown from contacting her could be relaxed. He had been banned from being within 50 yards of her, or 10 yards if at a public event, for his five years' probation. By modifying the restraining order, he would be able to have contact with RiRi again as long as he did not 'annoy, molest or harass her.'

Some people objected to Rihanna's decision, which confused her a little as she was the one who had been attacked by Chris, not them. She tweeted that she didn't care about the restraining order, and went on to talk to *Rolling Stone* magazine about it, telling the magazine: 'You can never please people, that's my decision. It doesn't mean we're getting married tomorrow. It doesn't mean we're gonna be in a relationship, or make up, or even talk ever again. It just means I didn't want to object to the judge.

'What he did to me was a personal thing, it had nothing to do with his career. Saying [he can't perform at awards shows] definitely made it difficult for him.'

In allowing the restraining order to be dropped to Level 1, RiRi wasn't inviting Chris to be involved in her life again, she was just letting him get on with his musical career.

Just a couple of days after the press broke the news of Rihanna's decision, she was on stage again, performing at the Grammy Awards on 13 February. That night, she was nominated for four awards of her own, along with another two for the songwriters of 'Love The Way You Lie'.

'Love The Way You Lie' was nominated for both Record of the Year and Song of the Year (songwriters' award) but was beaten both times by the Lady Antebellum track, 'Need You Now'. Eminem and RiRi were up for 'Best Rap/Sung Collaboration' and 'Best Rap' (songwriters' award) but lost out to Jay-Z and Alicia Keys for 'Empire State Of Mind'. In the 'Short Form Music Video' category they were beaten by Lady Gaga's 'Bad Romance'.

RiRi did triumph, though, in the 'Best Dance Recording' category with 'Only Girl (In the World)'. She also performed 'What's My Name?' for the first time with Drake, and 'Love the Way You Lie (Part II)' with Eminem. Afterwards, she tweeted: 'CONGRATULATIONS #RihannaNavy!!!! We

won a Grammy for BEST DANCE RECORDING!!!Only
ho in the woooorrrrrlllldddd!!!!'

When Eminem collected the Best Rap Album award for
'Recovery' he thanked RiRi, saying: 'I wanna thank
Rihanna, too, for helping to propel the album to where it's
at now.'

On 20 February 2011, Rihanna turned 23. Her best
celebrity pal Katy Perry wasn't able to be there because she
was on tour, but lots of her other friends and family helped
her celebrate. RiRi tweeted fans: 'Go grawl, its ya birthday,
ITS PARTY TIME! All my best friends are here!!!! And my
BRO!! Wish u cud see how SICK this s**t is!!!' Katy was
upset that she missed it, and tweeted: 'Happy birthday boo.
Wish I could b there to blackout! Luv U!'

But RiRi didn't want Katy to feel bad and tweeted back:
'Bitch are u kidding? I missed ur WEDDING!! This is small
stuff boo! #whenworkcalls.'

Rihanna actually performed at the NBA All-Star Weekend
on her birthday, but she had lots of fun entertaining the
crowds. She sang 'Umbrella', 'Rude Boy' and 'Only Girl (In
the World)', then Drake came on stage and sang 'What's My
Name?'. As he was singing, he wished her a happy birthday
and she got all giddy. Her final track was 'All Of The Lights'
with Kanye West.

Afterwards, she watched the game with Justin Bieber
and Lenny Kravitz, and then jumped into a car and
rushed to a party back at her house. She had time to get
changed and tuck into some special red velvet cupcakes
with the Barbados flag on top before her guests started

to arrive. Rihanna spent time with her closest friends before going on to the main party room to mingle with her celebrity friends. P. Diddy, Jay-Z, Beyoncé and Mary J.Blige all wanted to make sure RiRi had the best birthday ever.

Zac Efron, Rya Phillippe, Ce Lo Green and Christina Milian were there too, and Snoop Dog arrived late at around 1am. RiRi loved the trouble people had gone to, and posed for photos next to two special ice sculptures. One was of a column decorated with the letter 'R' and a crown, and the other was a giant fish. There was a huge display of around 30 jars of different sweets and lollipops for the guests to help themselves, and they partied until the early hours.

The day after her birthday, lots of media outlets started to say that what Rihanna wore for her NBA All-Star game performance was inappropriate for a family audience. They objected to her wearing fishnet stockings, and said that she grabbed her crotch during one song.

Usher knows how the media can twist things, and he defended RiRi's birthday performance during his interview on the *Loose Women* TV show. He declared: 'Artistic direction is just that, you know, and obviously subjective. Everyone has their opinion and it's a family show. I think she is a responsible young lady, and maybe the song represented the attitude of, you know, think about it like this: how long have guys been grabbing their crotches?'

The next day RiRi had some good news, as the President

of Mercury Music Group in the UK released an official statement saying she had sold over 10 million records in the UK alone, and was the first female artist to have No. 1 singles for five consecutive years. Jason Iley said: 'It was clear to me from the first time that I met Rihanna that she had the potential to be one of the most successful artists in the world.

'It has been a privilege to work with her these past six years. I believe that we have only seen the tip of the iceberg, and I'm looking forward to seeing her achieve even greater success in the coming months and years.'

Naturally, Rihanna doesn't like it when people say nasty things about her, and when she found out that 'Speechless' singer Ciara had been negative about her during an appearance on *Joan Rivers' Fashion Police* show, she decided to fight back.

Ciara had been asked to give her opinion on the dress Rihanna wore for the Brit Awards, when she commented: 'I ran into her recently at a party and she wasn't the nicest. It's crazy because I've always loved and respected what she's done with fashion and I've ran into her before, but this time it wasn't the most pleasant run-in.'

RiRi used Twitter to ask Ciara: 'My bad ci, did I 4get to tip u? #howrudeofme.'

Ciara responded: 'Trust me Rhianna u dont want to see me on or off stage,' but this was a foolish thing to say because it seemed to make RiRi more angry. She shot back: 'U gangsta huh? Haaa. Good luck with bookin that stage u speak of.'

Things soon calmed down and the girls decided to let bygones be bygones. RiRi tweeted. 'Ciara baby, I love u girl! You hurt my feelings real bad on TV! I'm heartbroken! That's y I retaliated this way! So sorry! #letsmakeup.' Ciara replied: 'Rih u know its always been love since day 1! Doing shows/everything. you threw me off in that party! Apology accepted. Let's chat in person.'

Once their little disagreement was over, RiRi could get on with celebrating the fact that her YouTube VEVO channel had just passed the billion views mark. This was a great achievement and proved how popular all her videos are, because their combined views made Rihanna the fourth artist ever to reach such a landmark amount. The only other artists to have previously achieved a billion views had been Eminem, Justin Bieber and Lady Gaga.

MOST POPULAR RIHANNA VIDEOS AT THE BILLION VIEWS MARK (APPROX.):

1. 'Rude Boy' – 140 million
2. 'Don't Stop The Music' – 137 million
3. 'What's My Name?' – 130 million
4. 'Only Girl (In the World)' – 106 million

At this stage, her collaboration with Eminem on his track 'Love The Way You Lie' had reached almost 300 million views on his VEVO channel.

After celebrating *Loud* going platinum in the US after selling one million copies, Rihanna decided to ask her fans which single she should release next. Up until then, she had sold 3.5 million copies of the album worldwide.

She tweeted her 3.7 million followers the message: 'QUESTION EXISTING: I'm shootin a new vid in a cpl wks, I just need u to tell me, which song should I shoot? What is my next single? its hard to go from s+m to SKIN! Don't wanna be 2 swiney.'

Her fans jumped at the opportunity to tell RiRi what they thought, and the tracks that received the most votes were 'Raining Men', 'Man Down', 'Cheers' and 'California King Bed'.

Once she'd seen what the fans wanted RiRi posted: 'K so its lookin like Man Down, CKB, Fadin, Cheers! But this was the EXACT problem I had b4, I can't choose between these 4 songs!

'Helllp!!! Ok, now gimme de top 2 in order of how they should be released! Remember its spring/ summertime!!!! See why I had to ask u guys??? SO HARD to choose.'

Even after lots of fans replied she still didn't know which song would be the best, tweeting: 'Man, I love CKB, But Man Down is so GANGSTA! Like dance hall queen type gangsta.

'And Cheers makes me wanna get chocolate wasted!! Whether its the weekend or NOT.'

In the end, she weighed them all up and decided to release both 'California King Bed' and 'Man Down'.

RiRi first performed 'California King Bed' as a duet with Sugarland's Jennifer Nettles at the Academy of Country Music Awards on 3 April 2011. She then did a solo on *American Idol*, with Nuno Bettencourt on guitar, and received a standing ovation from the judges. Everyone watching in the studio and at home was completely captivated, with many fans saying it was her best live performance to date.

She hired Anthony Mandler to direct the video, and he teased fans by tweeting: 'emotional light.....raw, and inspiring. Ckb.' He didn't give any more info but it was later reported that Jay-Z watched the video being filmed, and RiRi handpicked the male model she wanted to star as her lover. She had two models to choose from, and she picked one called Nathan because he had the best abs. RiRi's outfit for the video was sexy underwear, as the video is based in a bedroom, and she is caressing her lover on the bed.

The video was partly paid for by the skincare brand Nivea, because RiRi is the main face of their 100th anniversary campaign. They would use the song in their advertising campaign and be sponsoring her tour as well. All in all, they would spend $1.5 billion on the marketing campaign. The first promotional photo that she did for them was one with her topless, with her arms crossed, covering her breasts. She had no make-up on and was just showing her natural beauty.

In the official statement to announce the campaign, Markus Pinger from Nivea said: 'Over the past 100 years,

NIVEA has been an iconic skincare brand across the world that is built on the trust of our consumers.

'We are excited to have Rihanna supporting us in our celebration and building a new generation of fans.'

NEW ROLES

Lots of people have suggested that the next movie RiRi should be in is a remake of the Whitney Houston and Kevin Costner classic, *The Bodyguard*. The story is currently being brought up to date as Warner Bros have hired Jeremiah Friedman and Nick Palmer to write a new script. RiRi was reported to be shortlisted for the part, but in March 2011 she told *OK! Magazine* that there was no chance she would be appearing in the movie.

She said: 'I hate it when singers do singing movies all the time, because you can never look at them as anybody else.

'I want to play a character. My whole life is playing Rihanna, being a singer [in a movie] won't be a stretch for me. I like challenges and being an actor is playing a role, being able to step into somebody else's shoes, that's the excitement.'

In saying she wouldn't play the new Rachel Marron, Rihanna is proving that she wants to be a serious actress: she doesn't want easy parts.

She has also been linked to a remake of *The Last Dragon*, which is due for release in 2012. The original movie came out in 1985. The producer RZA said as long ago as December 2008 that he wanted Rihanna to play the TV music video host Laura Charles, and at the start of 2011, reports in the media suggested that she had agreed and would be starring in the film.

THE LAST TIME

The final day of the 'Last Girl On Earth Tour' took place in Perth, Australia on 12 March 2011. Rihanna had been touring for eleven months, but it must have been sad for her to perform her last concert. She knew she would be on the road again soon as her *Loud* tour was starting in June, but it wouldn't be the same. Most of her crew and dancers would stay with her, but some had come to the end of their journey with Rihanna and would be moving on to different projects.

Finishing in Australia had been nice, because RiRi had loved being in that country. She did find it strange that no-one she met there was the same colour as her, telling chat show host Chelsea Handler that she hadn't seen many black people in Australia and the few she had seen in her audiences had been very dark.

When the tour came to an end, some of RiRi's dancers and members of her band decided to film a thank-you video for her. They used clips of RiRi performing as well as backstage clips, and recorded special messages to create a video that would no doubt be treasured. In all, they had done a total of 73 shows together worldwide.

Dancer Chase Benz was the first to thank Rihanna in the video. He said: 'Robyn, what's up? It's Chase, I wanna say a few words, thank yous. I wanna say thank you for this year: it's been amazing, all the stuff you've done for us, as a whole crew, for me – you let me propose to my wife, that was a dream come true for me. It's also been a dream come true for me to dance behind such an amazing artist like yourself. And try not to get too teary-eyed with this one, but this year has been unbelievable, so hope you don't forget me. Hope to see you again soon. Thank you from the bottom of my heart.'

Eric Smith, her bassist and musical director, was the next person to leave his own message for Rihanna. He said: 'I just wanna say thanks: it's been incredible, working with you since the beginning, basically. Like I told you in Prayer, to watch you grow from a little girl to a grown woman on and off the stage, it's been incredible. You are amazing, A1, top of your game! I'm proud to say I'm your band leader, bass player and your big brother.'

Chris Johnson, RiRi's drummer, apologised in his message, commenting: 'I will say it was my mistake ever leaving you the first time. Coming back this time I've realised how much fun and how much of a great artist you are to work with. If you ever need anything, on, off the stage, just let me know.'

The last person to leave a message was Bryan Tanaka, another of RiRi's dancers. He spoke direct to RiRi through the camera, telling her: 'It's been amazing working with you for the past four years and to see you grow into a superstar in front of my eyes, just to see you turn into one of the most amazing singers and performers. The crowd love you; just being part of it, and working with you so closely for this long is definitely a blessing in my life, it's a big blessing. So I want to thank you very much from the bottom of my heart and it's been absolutely amazing to be like a bro to you, because I care about you: you're absolutely amazing at what you do! I'm looking forward to the future.'

On her return to the US, Rihanna joined with other singers, actors and sports personalities to promote the UNICEF Tap project. The aim of the campaign was to educate people so that they realised that 900 million others around the world don't have access to clean, safe water and to encourage them to do something about it.

The idea was that restaurant owners would back the Tap project, and start charging a dollar whenever a customer wants a glass of tap water; the money raised would be used to help give those in need access to clean water, and so reduce the number of people dying from waterborne diseases. On one of the adverts Rihanna poses with a bottle of water, which states: 'Rihanna Tap Water. Not your typical tap water, unless of course you live next door to Rihanna'.

She also filmed a video, which sees her drinking some tap water in a 'sexy' way.

As well as appearing in adverts, Rihanna also bottled some tap water from her own house, which people who donated to the cause could win. Her bottle was one of six to be included in the 'Celebrity Tap Pack' prize box, along with bottles from Selena Gomez, Taylor Swift, Robin Williams, Adrian Granier and Dwight Howard. For every $5 that fans donated at www.celebritytap.org, they could have one entry into the draw to win the celebrity water.

After the terrible earthquake and tsunami hit Japan on 11 March 2011, Rihanna wanted to do something to help: she always believes that she should use her celebrity status for good and supports many charities. Universal Music contacted her, and said they wanted to release an album of tracks to raise money for the Japanese people affected by the disaster. RiRi knew she had to get involved. She joined with U2, Bon Jovi, Nicki Minaj and 32 other recording artists to support the *Songs for Japan* album. Rihanna sang 'Only Girl (In the World)' and waived her royalties, as did the other artists taking part.

On the 28 April 2011 RiRi headed to New York for the DKMS 5th Annual Linked Against Leukaemia gala. She was presented an award by Katharina Harf, one of the co-founders of DKMS, for the work she has done to get more people to register to become bone marrow donors and the help she has given to people with leukaemia. Rihanna really is one in million.

Since splitting with Matt Kemp, Rihanna has been linked

with many people. She just needs to be at the same event as someone, and the media starts saying they were seen flirting and kissing! When she appeared on the Graham Norton chat show, she shared his sofa with *Phone Booth* actor Colin Farrell, comedian Rhod Gilbert and English actor Daniel Radcliffe.

Websites and blogs started to suggest that Rihanna and Farrell had been exchanging sexy text messages, and when they were both spotted enjoying a meal at the Los Angeles restaurant Giorgio Baldi in March 2011, people started to suggest they had been on a date. They had actually been sitting nowhere near each other and Farrell had been there for business, not to meet Rihanna.

Gossip sites also linked Rihanna to *Cruel Intentions* actor Ryan Phillippe only a month earlier, because he went to a few of the same events as her and attended her birthday party. The press tried to say they were keeping their relationship a secret, but Rihanna is supposed to have denied anything is going on between them to a member of the paparazzi. According to ITN, when she was asked whether she was dating Ryan, she said: 'No, no, no! I hate to burst your bubble, but no. I am dating girls – I am just kidding!'

AMERICAN
X FACTOR

When the news first broke that Simon Cowell planned to launch a US version of *The X Factor*, people everywhere started to wonder who he might pick to be the judges. Rihanna was one of the most popular choices but it wasn't to be. In fact, RiRi ruled herself out of the running because she wouldn't be able to spare the time to do the show; she would be too busy with her *Loud* tour from June 2011 onwards. She loves the UK show, and if it were at all possible, she would have jumped at the chance to be involved with mentoring the contestants in the US version.

One member of her 'family' did sign up to be a judge, though: L.A. Reid. He was willing to give up his job as chairman of Island Def Jam to be the other male judge on the show. His farewell letter to his staff was posted on the website Billboard.biz and read:

'Great leaders are almost always great simplifiers,
who can cut through argument, debate and doubt, to
offer a solution everybody can understand.'
Colin Powell

To my Island Def Jam family:
 After much consideration, I have decided to leave my
position as Chairman of the Island Def Jam Music
Group.
 I have always thrived on growth and the next great
challenge, and I look forward with much enthusiasm
to what the future holds.
 I am extremely proud of our beautiful roster and all
we have accomplished in my seven years with IDJ. We
continue to have incredible success together with
today's most phenomenal superstars – Rihanna, Justin
Bieber, Mariah Carey, Kanye West, Bon Jovi, Jennifer
Lopez, Ne-Yo, Rick Ross, The Killers, The-Dream,
Chrisette Michele, Jeezy and Ludacris, to name a few.
 I want to thank all of you for your amazing
contributions.
With Warm Regards –
L.A.

L.A. Reid might have left Island Def Jam but he will
continue to play a big part in RiRi's life, as he has been
part of the 'family' she established on moving to the US. It
is clear that she means a lot to him by the fact that he listed
her first out of the 13 artists he mentions in his farewell

letter: he has seen her develop from the shy girl who walked into his office into the world–class performer she is today.

Back in 2009, he told MTV: '[Rihanna is a] beautiful person. Internally, she has the right spirit. She makes great records, and I'm proud of her. Really proud of her.'

YOU WERE SLEEPING
NEXT TO ME

For the first performance of 'California King Bed', Rihanna decided to go for a totally new look. She asked her personal hairstylist Ursula Stephen to give her a pixie crop, and debuted her latest style at the Academy of Country Music Awards in Las Vegas on April 3. Ursula explained what had made RiRi want to go much shorter to *InStyle* magazine. She said: 'We haven't done a bob in a while, but the idea to go short was Rihanna's.

'She texted me a couple days prior to the ACM Awards and said she wanted to do something short. She missed her face, and I did too!'

Ursula set about cutting and styling RiRi's hair just the way she wanted it, and observed: 'We're not committed to anything but having fun!'

'California King Bed' was to be the sixth single released

from 'Loud' in the USA, and was the fourth single elsewhere. RiRi shot the video in March on a stage in West Hollywood, Los Angeles. She only had a day to shoot it because she was so busy. The video has a romantic feel and setting. The majority of the video sees RiRi in an outside bedroom by the beach. She is seen lying on some ornamental grass, on the bed, caressing her love interest, sitting on a chair, playing with the drapes around the room and standing against a stone wall.

The video was directed by Anthony Mandler and it is similar in style to the 'Only Girl (In the World)' video. Anthony told MTV: 'I think it's something that is so unique about Rihanna whatever she's doing, whatever character she's playing, whatever side of herself she's showing, she's in it 1,000 per cent... And I think the song and the theme of this song, she wanted to obviously show a softer side, a lighter side, one that's caught in maybe a tumultuous relationship... There's so much variety with her and it's been such a journey with her.'

He also directed the video for 'Man Down', and confessed: 'We've done sixteen videos together... and what we're coming with next is certainly gonna flip peoples' minds with 'Man Down'. We shot the video last month in Jamaica and it's my favourite song she's ever recorded, so I was really excited to get involved.

'And it's just one of those songs that demands a strong narrative and visual, and let's just say she let me go all the way. So I think you can expect something that's dramatic and shocking and intense and emotional and uplifting and enlightening... Without saying too much, if you're looking for a narrative you're not going to be disappointed, just know that it's going to be exciting.'

RiRi wanted to shoot both videos close together because many fans love 'Man Down' and 'California King Bed' equally. She tweeted: 'JAMAICA was the BEST!!!!! #RihannaNavy its a big month for u guys! TWO #MAJAH videos droppin' #whosLOUD. They're both very different! One is #GAWJUS and the other is a MOVIE. RIHquest Man Down and California King Bed on your favourite radio station.'

On 12 April, the finalists for the 2011 Billboard Awards were announced, with Rihanna leading the pack with 18 nominations. RiRi was up for Top Artist, Top Social Artist, Top Hot 100 Artist, Top Digital Songs Artist, Top Radio Songs Artist, Top Streaming Artist, Top Digital Media Artist, Top Female Artist, Top R&B Artist, Top Dance Artist, Top R&B Song (for 'What's my Name?' featuring Drake) and Top R&B Album (for Loud). For 'Love The Way You Lie' with Eminem she was up for six awards: Top Hot 100 Song, Top Digital Song, Top Radio Song, Top Streaming Song (audio), Top Streaming Song (video) and Top Rap Song.

She was also going to be opening the show on 22 May, and told Ryan Seacrest she was to sing 'S & M'. She was also planning a big surprise for her fans – a duet with Britney Spears!

On the night itself, RiRi decided to wear a white men's Max Azria suit with the front of the shirt completely undone on the red carpet. She didn't stop smiling all night as she picked up the awards for Top Female Artist, Top Radio Songs Artist and Top Rap Song for 'I Love The Way You Lie'. Her performance of 'S & M' had the audience captivated, and she wore a white bodysuit with a chain running from her wrists. Her dancers stayed underneath the platform for the majority of the performance with their hands and arms reaching upwards to try and touch her. Britney appeared, wearing a black body suit complete with bunny mask, and they each danced with a pole before having a pillow fight with a few of RiRi's dancers.

BRITNEY
SPEARS

If you had told RiRi at the start of 2011 that she would have performed 'S & M' with Britney she wouldn't have believed it. Back then she knew that she wanted to do an 'S & M Remix', but she wasn't sure who she wanted to do it with and so she asked her fans on Twitter.

She had already dreamed about asking Britney Spears, and so when she received a lot of the votes for the 'Femme Fatale' singer, she knew it was the right way to go. She then had to find a way of approaching Britney…

On 10 April 2011, RiRi's Twitter followers were the first to know that Britney Spears would be collaborating with Rihanna on the 'S & M Remix'. RiRi tweeted: 'I got a #SEXY collabo comin your way supa dupa soon!!!! OH YEAH!!! By popular demand….'

'It's BRITNEY BITCH!!!!'

'@britneyspears one of the biggest worldwide popstars! U gangsta #EPIC'

'MAJAH Rihmix to S&M MAJAH!!!! #S&Mrihmix #itsBRITNEYbitch'

Britney tweeted back:

@rihanna You're such a tease! I like it, like it…. – Britney

@rihanna You think they're ready Ri Ri?… – Britney

As soon as the news broke that Britney was to feature on the 'S & M Remix', everyone wanted to know how Rihanna managed to persuade her to do it. When RiRi was doing a radio interview with DJ Lil Cee on 92.3 NOW FM, he asked her the question and she replied: 'I always wanted to work with her – I just thought it would be so unexpected for two artists in the same genre like that to collaborate – and Britney, she's never been featured on any one else's record ever, so when she heard that we were interested in doing a remix and we wanted her to do it, she was really enthusiastic about it. She loved the idea and she went right into the studio.'

The whole process, from inviting Britney to do it, to recording the track and for it to come out, took less than a week.

Two days after the remix of 'S & M' was released, it topped the US iTunes chart. Rihanna was really happy, as she tweeted her followers: '#1 on ITUNES!!! WOW, u lil rascals! WE love u.'

'I wanna BIG UP all the #MAJAH Rihanna+Britney fans for coming together and supporting #S&MRihmix in such an EPIC way! Thank u'

She had also just become the second female artist to have a fan page on Facebook, with 30 million likes. Overall, her page was the seventh most popular:

1. Texas Hold'em Poker fan page
2. Facebook fan page
3. Eminem
4. Lady Gaga
5. Michael Jackson
6. YouTube
7. Rihanna

The 'S & M Remix' became Rihanna's tenth No. 1, and Steve Bartels, president and COO of the Island Def Jam Music Group, released the following statement in response: 'Rihanna's tenth #1 single is a monumental accomplishment and a testament to her incredible artistry.

'This was a truly collaborative and creative effort, spearheaded by Rihanna's tireless work and aided in no small part by the incredible Britney Spears and her team. I am extremely proud of Rihanna, her ongoing dominance on the charts, and the entire IDJ team who worked so diligently to bring this one home.'

RiRi also broke a chart record when 'S & M Remix' went to No. 1, because she was the youngest artist to ever have ten No. 1 singles on the Hot 100 charts. Previously, the record was held by Mariah Carey (who had been 25 years, eight months and one week old when she celebrated her tenth No. 1 in December 1995) – Rihanna was only

23 years, two months and one week old. She also broke the record for the quickest time between a solo artist's first and tenth No. 1 single as it only took her four years, 11 months and two weeks. The previous record holder was also Mariah Carey.

This was all achieved without a music video to accompany the track, something that is quite unheard of. Fans of both RiRi and Britney wanted a video to be made, and for a while it looked as if there was going to be one, but this proved to be just a rumour.

Ryan Seacrest set the record straight on his radio show, telling listeners: 'We decided to investigate it – I can tell you the rumours are 100 per cent false. If you want them to change their minds, tweet Rihanna and tweet Britney – don't tell them I told you to do it!'

HOME

In April 2011, Rihanna moved into her first proper home, after purchasing a modernist mansion in Los Angeles. It has 12 bedrooms, and so she always has room for her family and friends to stay over when they visit her; it was also extremely expensive.

She revealed to *Vogue*: 'I looked steady for two years, and it is way above the price I was looking for, but I loved it.'

RiRi enjoyed being able to decorate it in just the way she liked, and added: 'It is all white – there is a gun chandelier in the middle of the living room. In one room, I have this huge black-and-white painting of Bob Marley, and the wallpaper is green, yellow and red, the African flag colours.'

She won't be living there on her own, though. RiRi now has her own baby: her toy poodle Oliver, who lives with the singer and her best friend Melissa Forde. In the last place they shared, Rihanna received so much fan mail that she had to give it a whole room in her house! The former theatre room became her fan-mail room, and she filled it with letters, drawings and gifts that fans have sent her over the years. She receives loads of stuff every day from all around the world. It's a good job she has so many bedrooms, because she might need two or three to store her fan mail; she keeps getting more and more each day.

Quite a few of RiRi's friends are older than her, but it's no surprise really; she behaves much older than she is. She explained to *W Magazine*: 'I've been paying my own bills since I was 17, living in a foreign country, and I've always been a little older than my real age. People always said that to me, and I always felt that in my head.'

The 'Loud Tour' is set to become Rihanna's biggest-ever tour, as she is doing 88 dates from 4 June to 22 December 2011. Originally, it was going to be smaller than the 'Last Girl on Earth Tour' (which had 73 dates), but so many fans wanted to go that Rihanna added more dates. She didn't want people to miss out, and sold more than 300,000 tickets in the UK alone. RiRi also broke the record for the O2 Arena, as no other solo artist has ever performed 10 shows there: normally, they just perform one or two.

She said in a statement: 'We're creating an incredible ride with this tour. I'm excited to get out on the road and share my new music from this album. We are going to have an amazing time and I know my fans are ready to get LOUD!'

As well as performing lots of tracks from her *Loud* album,

Rihanna also made sure 'Disturbia' and 'Umbrella' were part of her set list, as she loves performing them and fans love them, too – they are big fan favourites.

RiRi wanted her concert to be the best her fans had ever seen, and so as soon as the tour was announced in December 2010, she started working with her creative team on the new set and costume designs. She also wanted the best supporting act, and was thrilled when J. Cole signed up to come on tour with her. Cee Lo Green, singer of the Gnarls Barkley smash hit 'Crazy', originally signed on for some dates, but unfortunately had to pull out because of a scheduling conflict.

Back in February 2011, RiRi told *Extra*: 'I'm really excited about [the "Loud Tour"]. We're just starting to put it together and it's going to be even bigger than my last tour, which I didn't think [was possible]. The "Loud Tour" is going to be special.'

In another interview with Ryan Seacrest, she said: 'We're going to start the first week in June in the United States. It's the *Loud* era, so I'm very excited! It's going to be new colours, new stage and a new show...'

She added in a later interview with Ryan: 'We've just designed the stage and we have a section that we are building where the fans can actually be in the show and in the stage, and be closer than they've ever been. It's real VIP!'

When some websites started to spread the rumour that some of RiRi's tour dates might have to be cancelled because of poor ticket sales, she was understandably upset. There was no truth in the stories, as all of Rihanna's tour dates were proving popular and looked like they would be sell-outs.

On most nights of the tour, the set list ran as follows:

1. Video Introduction
2. 'Only Girl (In the World)'
3. 'Disturbia'
4. 'Shut Up and Drive'
5. 'Man Down'
6. 'Darling Nikki'
7. 'S&M'
8. 'Let Me'
9. 'Skin'
10. 'Raining Men'
11. 'Hard'
12. 'Breakin' Dishes'
13. 'The Glamorous Life'
14. 'Medley: 'Run This Town' / 'Live Your Life'
15. 'Untitled IV' (Video Interlude)
16. 'Unfaithful'
17. 'Hate That I Love You'
18. 'California King Bed'
19. 'Untitled V' (Video Interlude)
20. 'What's My Name?'
21. 'Rude Boy'
22. 'Cheers (Drink to That)'
23. 'Don't Stop the Music'
24. 'Take a Bow'
25. Encore

Both critics and fans agree that RiRi's 'Loud' Tour is her best tour to date. Amanda Ash from the *Vancouver Sun* wrote in her review: 'Rihanna knows how to throw a party – a sexy, steamy, tight and bright bash where yesterday's troubles are crushed beneath mile-high stilettos and drowned by intoxicating club beats.'

Rihanna has achieved so much already but she wants to try some more things in the next few years. In the next 10 years she would like to have her own make-up and clothing lines. She is so passionate about fashion that having the opportunity to design clothes for other women would be a dream come true for her.

RiRi would also like to win more Grammys and other awards for her music, and release more hit singles. What matters to her the most, though is keeping her fans happy because they make everything she does worthwhile.

She is so thankful to everyone who has helped her get where she is today, and looks forward to what the future holds...